Print,
Make,
Wear

Author's dedication:
To my mother Stella

Published in 2015
by Laurence King Publishing Ltd
361–373 City Road
London EC1V 1LR
Tel +44 20 7841 6900
Fax +44 20 7841 6910
E enquiries@laurenceking.com
www.laurenceking.com

ISBN 978 178067 470 4

Designed by Jane Chipchase-Bates
Project Editor: Gaynor Sermon
Printed in China

Print, Make, Wear

Creative Projects for
Digital Textile Design

Melanie Bowles
and The People's Print

CONTENTS

DIGITAL DESIGN TUTORIALS

RESOURCES

FOREWORD

Once upon a time, if you wanted to print some fabric to make a new blouse you had to look in the telephone directory and cold call a printer who would tell you that, after a prohibitive set-up fee, they could offer you a minimum run of 500 metres. And that's if you were lucky! Of course, you didn't need 500 metres, you only needed two. The design you had in mind was lovely and original and you could really picture yourself wearing it, but with no way to print it you gave up and went to a high-street store instead. There, you'd end up buying a printed blouse that thousands of other people owned in order to temper your disappointment and frustration

At long last, this scenario is a thing of the past. Thanks to contemporary digital printing technology, there are now dozens of digital printers in many countries who print two metres of fabric at the click of a button and at an affordable cost. Melanie Bowles and The People's Print have created this book to allow you to develop inspirational projects and transform these into professional print-ready designs. The tutorials help you to avoid the pitfalls of making generic digitally printed fabrics using old-fashioned effects such as tile repeats and mirror tools. She enables you to fast track to sophisticated design, professional-level skills and new clothes that you, your friends and family will love. Gone are the days of hampered creativity!

There is also a much larger cultural implication and big-vision philosophy behind *Print Make Wear* that sits silently beneath the surface. This is a best-practice ethos with a nod to sustainable development and new 'maker models' developed over many years by the author (and The People's Print). An example of one such best practice aspect relates to DIY culture and consumer-centred design. Broadly speaking, this marks a cultural shift in consumers' attitudes by challenging the individual's relationship with passive consumerism and, in particular, the consumption of mass-produced fashion.

By giving the individual tools and know-how to make their own designs, prints and clothes (in an accessible and professional way), new ideas and methods of production are envisaged, new opportunities arise and new forms of industry and community are stimulated. This echoes past technological catalysts for spurring localized industry, for example the Spinning Jenny (the first mechanized spinning frame) in the eighteenth century and the domestic sewing machine in the nineteenth century, both of which transformed the textiles industry into entirely new, never-seen-before industrial enterprises.

The DIY design revolution that is at your fingertips in *Print Make Wear* promises a similar revolution – a contemporary catalyst for change, empowerment and enterprise – that promises to shift the fashion-making landscape into a new paradigm yet again.

Print Make Wear acts as a bridge between ideas and making, presented in an accessible, easy-to-follow way. As Melanie knows from her role as a senior lecturer in Printed Textiles at Chelsea College of Art and Design, much of art college training is about developing a sophisticated vision and aptitude for the process of ideation to realization in the students. Such precious knowledge is distilled in these pages – a boon for amateurs, professionals and graduates alike.

From a business point of view, the function of this book is multilayered. Not only does it stimulate exciting new opportunities for the printers, their suppliers, fans and clients, it creates new business opportunities for individual makers, supports young companies that have limited time to develop new CAD skills and stimulates the cottage industry businesses that are the backbone of so many economies. From a cultural point of view, the tutorials in this book stimulate people's skills during an era that at times has been fearful of losing its local craft, making and manufacturing skills. The stimulation of design and production skills is important in this case as it not only empowers people but if individuals produce things they are less

likely to see themselves as just consumers. Themes of textiles and sustainability arose through the fast pace of fashion consumption that increased exponentially over the last ten years (with retailers promoting dozens of fashion seasons each year). Such speed and its broad anti-sustainable effects were seen as so grave that even NGO organizations such as Greenpeace addressed them in 'Toxic Threads: The Big Fashion Stitch-Up'. The media has regularly reported on people who were throwing away their clothes after just one wearing or as soon as they were 'out of date'…

This is the contextual background from which *Print Make Wear* rises. Not only are the projects beautiful and inspiring, but they also present a new starting point from which to empower, enable and invigorate a counter-culture, bespoke fashion, new skills and exciting new maker communities.

Dr Emma Neuberg
www.thepeoplesprint.com

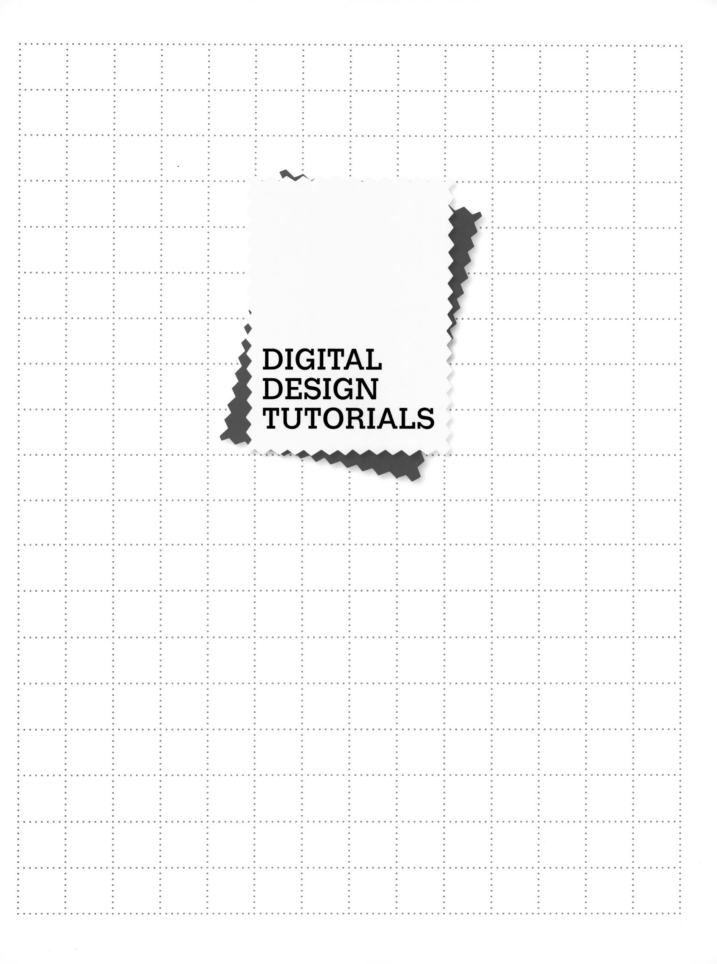

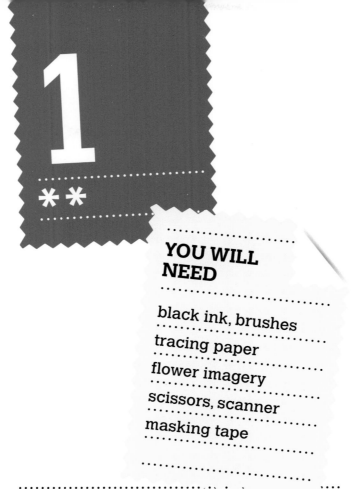

1
**

The Paintbrush Floral

Designer – Melanie Bowles

The Paintbrush Floral tutorial was designed for a workshop held by The People's Print, 'The Great British Floral', for the V&A Museum as part of the British Design Exhibition in 2012 and the Chelsea Flower Show. It is inspired by wild flowers and iconic Liberty floral prints. This tutorial shows you how to create your own paintbrush floral design using Photoshop. Print onto a fresh cotton poplin to make a floral skirt you will want to wear all summer long.

Getting Started

In this tutorial you'll build a paintbrush library to create floral designs. You will need images to trace from, and these can be found in books, magazines, postcards, greeting cards or photographs you have taken. Get inspired by traditional floral design such as famous Liberty prints.

Research

Start by creating a motif for each brush that you will use to produce your pattern. Print out any floral photos you have or refer to books of flowers.

With tracing paper and black ink, make a series of ink tracings.

Trace and paint

Choose a variety of scales, angles and shapes. The black silhouettes will form the paintbrushes which will create your floral designs. It is best to use a black motif to allow maximum definition when you come to build your design.

Scan in your drawings at 300 dpi to ensure a crisp outline.

Creating a brush

4

In Photoshop select the Magic Wand from the toolbar and select a motif.

5

Now you will create your brushes using the Brushes palette.
Edit > Define Brush
Name the brush and click OK.

Your new brush will be saved in the Brushes palette. You can create a series of brushes to play with in the same way.

6

Open the Brushes palette.
Window > Brush
Ensure that the Brush tool is active.

The Photoshop Brush Library provides extensive options to scale, rotate, scatter and colour your brushes. You are instantly able to create designs that have a hand rendered feel.

It is worth experimenting with these options to see what you might want to use.

Adding colour

 7

You are ready to introduce colour to your design. Use the Layers palette to apply colour to your flower motifs. Open a new document 12 x 12 cm (4¾ x 4¾ in) at 300dpi. Create a new layer so that you have the background layer free to change the base colour.

In your new layer select a flower brush. Apply colour and change the scale to fit your new document. Paint your motif by clicking once. Keep repeating this process until you have created a composition of poppies.

 8

You can add detail in the centres of the flowers. To stop your pattern looking flat, add variety using the Shape Dynamics tool. Open the Brushes palette and select Shape Dynamics. Change the Size Jitter and the Angle Jitter. Play with the sizes and angles by using the slide rule to alter the percentage jitter.

 9

Create a new layer for every flower to build your design so you can edit at any time.

Building a design

 10

Keep your flowers within the document unit. Don't put any flowers over the boundary edge.

 11

You can try out different background colours. Open the Layers palette and select Background. If you change the background colour remember to flatten the image:

Layers > Flatten Image

 12

Once you are happy with your floral design unit

Layer > Flatten Image

Your design is ready to use as a repeat unit.

ARTIST'S TIP

TO BREAK UP THE BACKGROUND COLOUR ADD SOME WHITE FLOWERS ON A NEW LAYER AND PLACE ABOVE THE BACKGROUND LAYER.

Ready for repeat

The next stage is to put the floral design into a simple half-drop repeat. You should aim for a continuous pattern with no breaks or interruptions. To create successful repeats in Photoshop, you need to be confident at mending seams.

Here's how you do it. Start by preparing your design unit.

View > Snap to > All
Edit > Select All
Edit > Free Transform

Drag ruler from the top of the document

Crosshairs will appear in the centre point of the design.

Drag a ruler so it clicks into place with the crosshair.

Hit Escape on your keyboard. Select All to copy your design
Edit > Copy

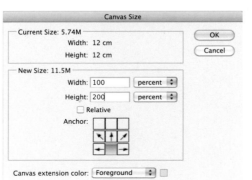

Image > Canvas Size
Select the middle box at the bottom of the Anchor grid. Change Height to 200 percent and click OK. You will see the canvas size double in height.

Repeat process

 16

Edit > Paste
Now move the pasted design so that the top snaps into place along the guide line. Flatten the image

Layers > Flatten Image
With your brushes fill in the seam that has appeared with new flowers. You can also use the Clone tool to copy flowers. Select it from the Options bar and select a soft brush. Choose the area you want to clone and press the Alt/Option key to set the copy target point. Move the Clone tool onto the seam and start mending.

Seam to be filled →

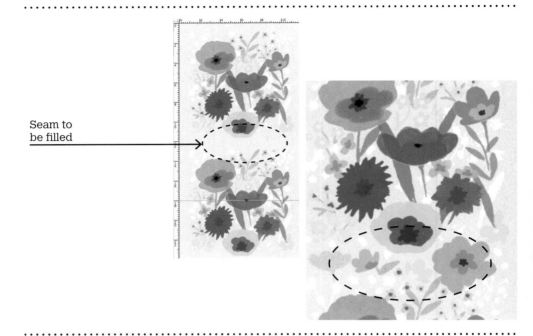

 17

With the seam filled your design begins to look continuous.

Select > All
Edit > Copy

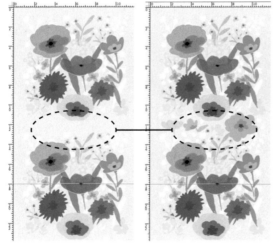

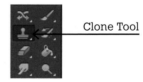

Clone Tool

 18

Image > Canvas Size
Select the middle left hand box. Change the Width to 200 percent.

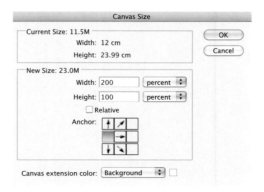

Mending seams

 19

<u>**Edit > Paste**</u>
Move the image so that the top snaps into place with the guidelines.

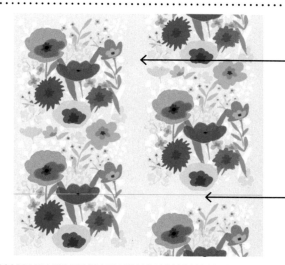

Seam to be filled ⟵

Seam to be filled ⟵

 20

Drag the design unit so the bottom snaps onto the guide line.
<u>**Layers > Flatten Image**</u>

Empty seams will appear that need to be filled with motifs.

 21

Now mend the seams as before using the brushes and Clone tool until all the empty seams are filled. You will begin to see the continuous pattern emerging.
<u>**Layers > Flatten Image**</u>

More mending

22

Now you are going to create a repeat using the Offset filter.
   Image > Image Size
Note the pixel measurements.

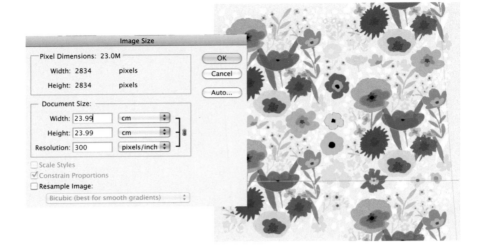

23

Filter > Other > Offset
Select Wrap Around. Divide the Horizontal and the Vertical pixel sizes by two and enter the new values. Click OK.

New seams will appear, and once again you will need to mend them. You can use the Clone tool to copy mended seams that you have already done.

24

With all the seams filled your design will be a continuous pattern.

YOU ARE NEARLY THERE!

Pattern fill

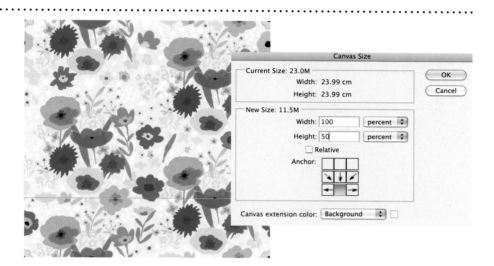

Image > Canvas Size
Select the middle square at the bottom.

Change Height to 50 percent. Click OK.

Your design is now in a half drop repeat. You can change the image size if you wish.

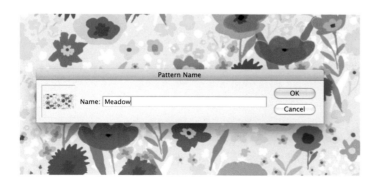

Your repeat unit is ready to be sent to the printer. Do a final check to see how the pattern flows.
Select > All
Edit > Define Pattern
We named our design 'Meadow'.

Open up a new document larger than your repeat image size to see the repeat effect.
Edit > Fill > Pattern
Select Pattern and find your new pattern.

More designs

Now that you know the technique you can create a whole collection of designs based on the Paintbrush Floral tutorial.

POPPY

CORNFLOWER

DANDELION

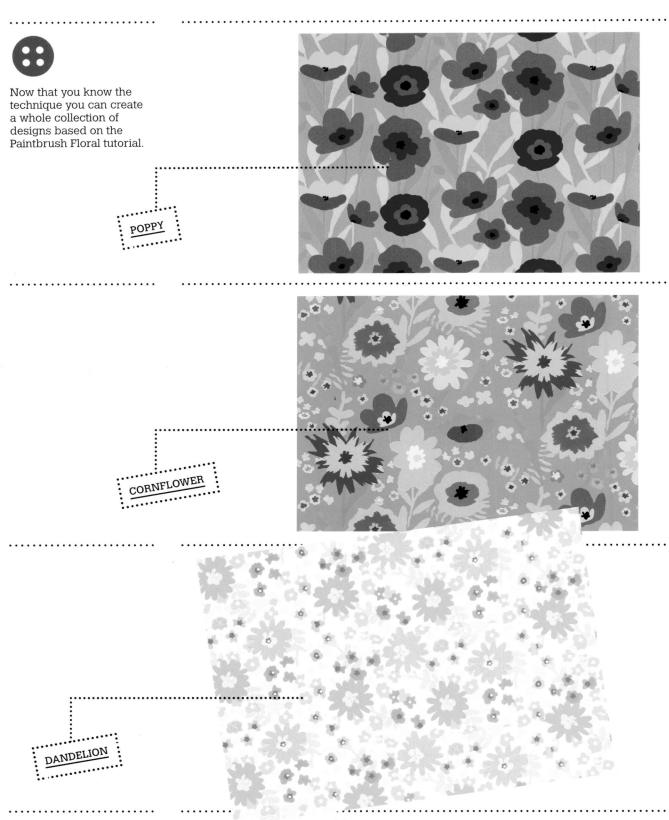

2

**

Post-Modern Play

Designer – Melanie Bowles

Inspired by the Post-Modernist movement, this tutorial shows you how to use Photoshop to create easy repeats which you can build into geometric patterns. You will use basic drawing tools and Pattern Fill tools to interlink and connect your pattern shapes to create a complex repeating pattern. Enter into the electric spirit of Post Modernism by digitally printing onto a plain cotton sweatshirt or slouch Tee.

Getting Started

Get inspired by the Post Modernist era of witty colour and spontaneous pattern. This tutorial shows you how to make quick patterns that interlock and look complex but only use basic Photoshop tools such as the Polygon Lasso and Define Pattern.

Drawing shapes

First experiment with cutting out shapes from origami paper.

Open Photoshop and a new document sized 40 x 40 cm (15¾ x 15¾ in) at 300dpi. Select the Polygon Lasso tool from the toolbar. With this tool draw the cut shapes that you made with your paper cutting.

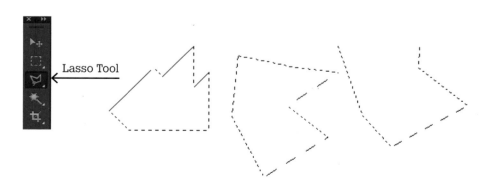

Lasso Tool

Building a pattern

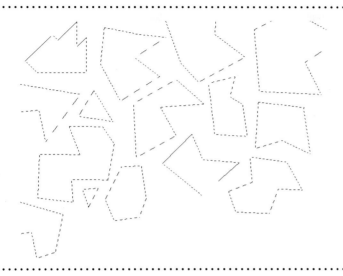

Continue to make shapes with the Polygon Lasso tool by holding down the Shift key as you build up shapes. Your shapes can go over the edge of the document to give a sense of a continuous pattern.

Once you have filled your document, fill your shapes with black
Edit > Fill > Foreground Colour

Pattern repeat

You will now put this basic design unit into repeat and add colour later. Jot down the image pixel size
Image > Image Size
In this case it is 4724 x 4724 pixels.

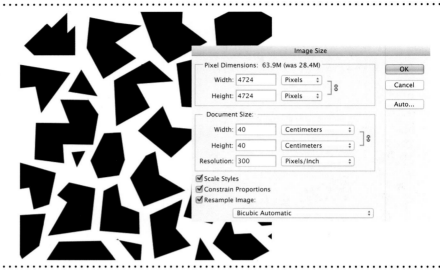

Now use the Offset filter to cut and flip the design ready to make it into a repeatable unit.
Filter > Other > Offset

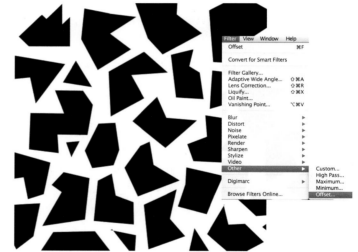

In the Offset dialogue box, divide the horizontal and the vertical pixel image sizes by two, enter the new values and click OK.

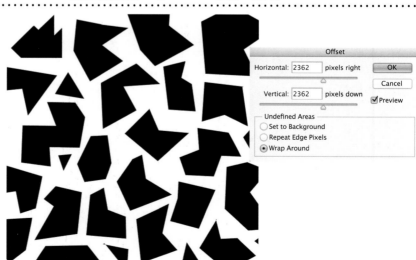

Mending seams

 7

Your design has now been cut into four and flipped around so the outside of the design is in repeat. You will notice seams appear: these need to be mended.

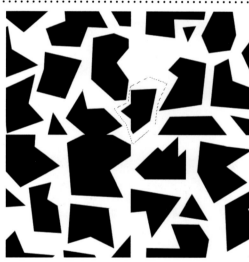

 8

To mend the seam between the repeat sections, select the Polygon Lasso tool from the toolbar and draw around the shapes that sit on the central seams.
Edit > Cut
Your shapes will be deleted from the seams.

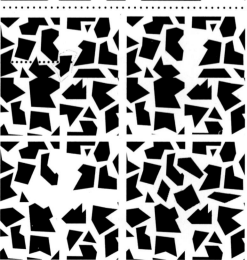

 9

Once you have deleted these shapes you can draw them back in using the Polygon Lasso tool.

ARTIST'S TIP
USING THE LASSO TOOL TO MAKE CUT SHAPES IS SO FAST AND FUN!

Applying colour

Your basic design unit is now in repeat. Save and name the document. It is a good idea to preserve this original file and continue to work on a copy so that you can always refer back to the original and use it as a template for further colour variations.

Now change the image size.
Image > Image Size
20 x 20 cm (8 x 8 in).

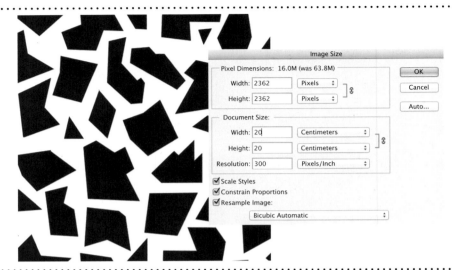

Colour in your shapes, referring to your cut paper shapes in coloured paper. Try to colour the edge shapes the same so that when they repeat they match. You can also check this using the Offset filter. Give the background layer a fill of blue.

Fill Tool

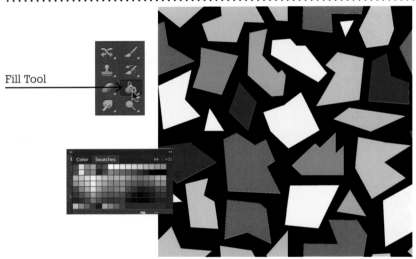

Remember that your design is already in repeat so, once coloured, make it into a pattern.
Edit > Define Pattern
This will save your first pattern fill to the Pattern Library which you will use later.

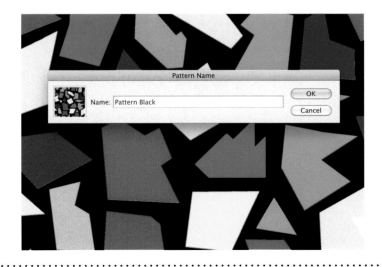

Different colourways

Now change the colour of the design unit. Change the colour of every shape so that they are different to the last colourway. Go to the background layer and change the colour.

As before
Edit > Define Pattern
You now have two pattern fills. Save and name them for future use.

Open your original design unit; this is 40 x 40 cm (15¾ x 15¾ in) and in repeat.

You also have two pattern fills of the same design but in different colourways and measuring 20 x 20 cm (7¾ x 7¾ in). These smaller repeat units will fit perfectly into the original unit. Select one shape with the Magic Wand.

From the Menu bar click
Select > Select Similar
to select all your black shapes.

Filling pattern

16

It's time to start filling in your shapes and building your design using the Pattern Fill tools. To start you will fill in the shapes in your design unit with one of your saved pattern fills.

Edit > Fill

In the Fill dialogue box select Pattern and find your first design unit under Custom Pattern.

Click OK.

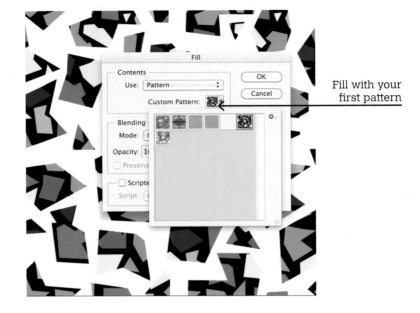

Fill with your first pattern

17

Now you are going to fill the white space with your other pattern. Your shapes are still selected, so just inverse the selection so the white space is selected. From the Menu bar click on

Select > Inverse

In the Fill dialogue box select Pattern and find your second design unit under Custom Pattern. Click OK.

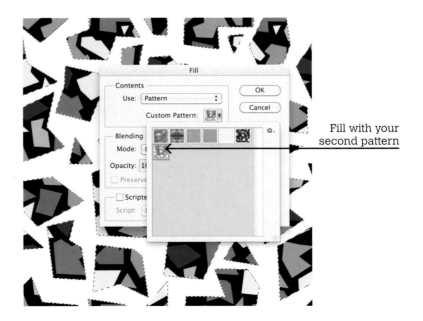

Fill with your second pattern

Pattern repeat

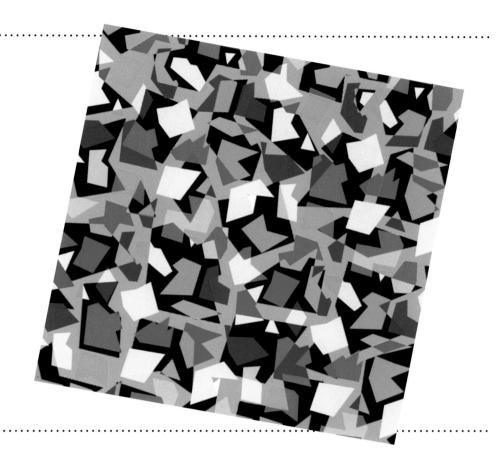

See how the pattern shapes interlink and connect to create a complex but repeating pattern.

Before you define as a final pattern you can change the image size.

YOUR PATTERN IS NOW COMPLETE!

Edit > Define Pattern
Name your design unit and click OK.

Pattern Name

Name: Post Modern Design

OK

Cancel

The final design

Open a new document 80 x 80 cm (31½ x 31½ in)
Edit > Fill > Pattern
Find your pattern and fill your new document to see how the design repeats.

Clever eh?!

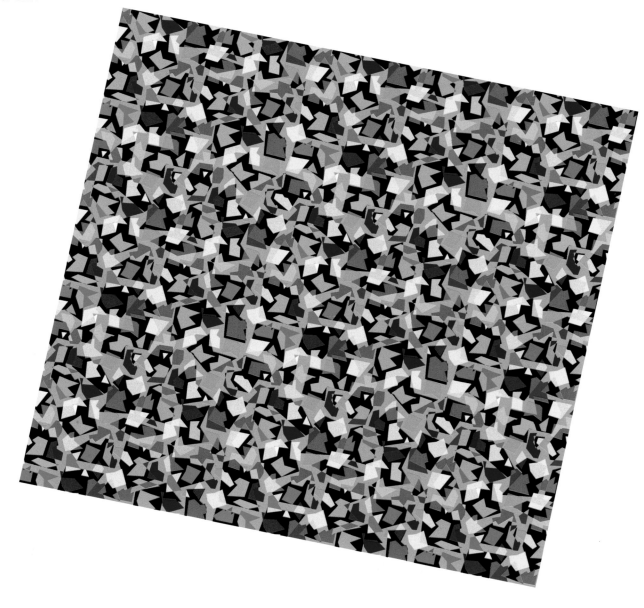

3

*

YOU WILL NEED

paper pad, scissors

thick marker pens

thin marker pens

ruler, scanner

Easy Boy Check

Designer – Melanie Bowles

Make your mark and create a unique signature check. In this tutorial you will use felt tip marker pens and simple flip and overlay techniques in Photoshop to create your very own check plaid pattern. Print the check onto a durable cotton poplin and make it into a classic men's shirt.

Getting Started

The inspiration for this design came from skateboard images. Look through magazines and websites for high-energy images and vibrant colours to build a check pattern with attitude.

Preparation

1

Cut a series of 10 x 10 cm (4 x 4 in) squares of paper. As they are small it makes it easier to draw nice free stripes that bleed over the edges. Use a ruler and pencil to mark the mid point of each square with a horizontal line to give you a rough guide for drawing your stripes.

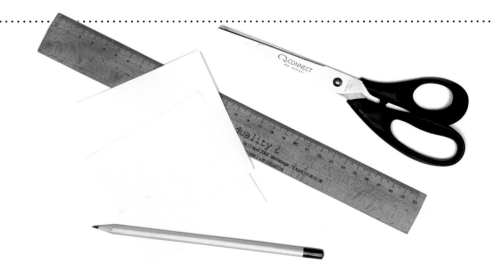

Drawing stripes

Use large felt tip markers to draw your stripes. At this stage, keep the stripes simple as you will be using the Layers tool in Photoshop to build a more complex check.

Create a series of stripe designs. It is nice to retain the imperfections and marks of the original felt tip markers.

Scanning

Scan your stripes into
Photoshop at 300dpi.
Save your scans.

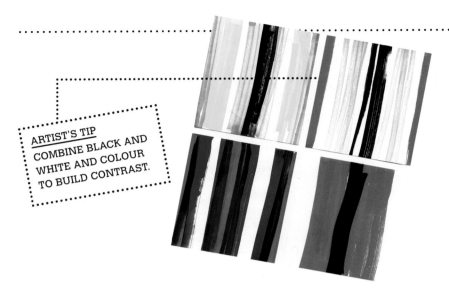

ARTIST'S TIP
COMBINE BLACK AND
WHITE AND COLOUR
TO BUILD CONTRAST.

In Photoshop open the
saved scan. With the
Marquee tool select
the drawing. To keep
the proportions of your
original drawing select and
hold down the Shift key.
   Edit > Copy

Open a new document 10 x
10 cm (4 x 4 in) at 300 dpi
   Edit > Paste
Your scanned stripe will
appear. Make sure it floods
the document – you may
need to enlarge it slightly:
   Edit > Transform > Scale
To lock it into position go to
   Layer > Flatten Image

Now you are ready to build
your Easy Boy Check.

Size & transform

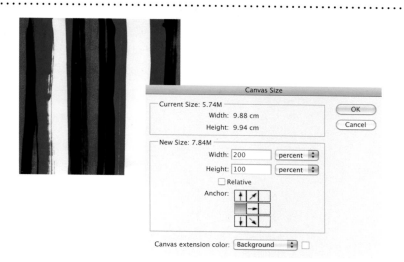

Canvas Size

Current Size: 5.74M
Width: 9.88 cm
Height: 9.94 cm

New Size: 7.84M
Width: 200 percent
Height: 100 percent
☐ Relative
Anchor:

Canvas extension color: Background

You are now going to build our stripe ready to create a check.

First make a copy of the stripe
Select > All
Edit > Copy
Image > Canvas Size
Select the middle left hand box and set the width to 200 percent.

In the toolbar make sure the background colour is set to white.

Click OK.

Your canvas width will double in size.

Edit > Paste
The copied stripe will appear.

At this point you can select Transform from the drop down menu to flip the square. This creates a mirror image
Edit > Transform > Flip Horizontal
Flatten the image:
Layer > Flatten Image

Flip

Now you need to repeat the process to create more stripes, but this time you will flip the design vertically.
Select > All
Edit > Copy

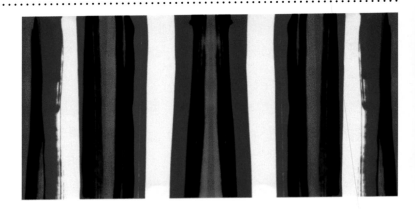

Image > Canvas Size
Select the top middle box of the Anchor grid. Increase the height to 200 percent.
Edit > Paste

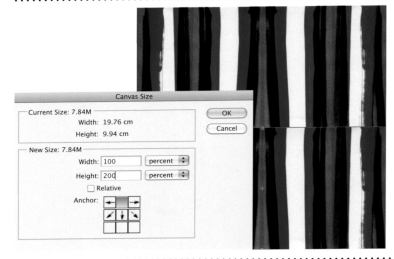

To mirror the design
Edit > Transform >
Flip Vertical
You will see a mirror image of your design appear.
Layer > Flatten Image

Building the check

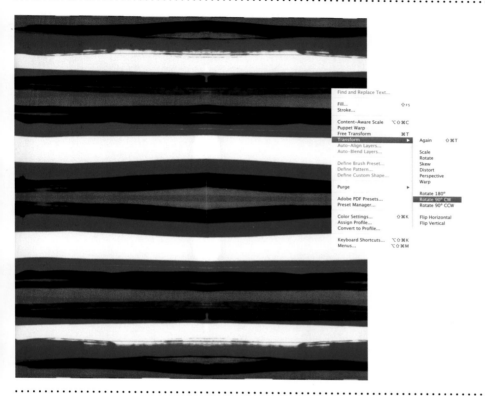

Now you will work with the Layers tools to create the check pattern.
Select > All
Edit > Copy
Edit > Paste
You will now have two layers.

With the top layer selected use the Transform tool to change the pattern rotation.
Edit > Transform > Rotate 90 CW

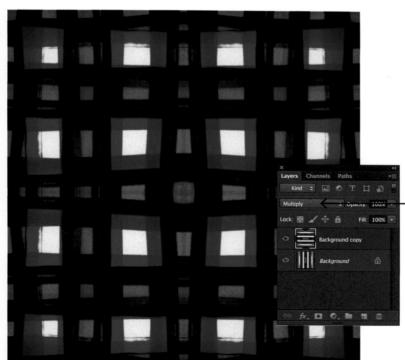

Blending Mode

To reveal the background layer and create the check, go into the Layers palette and change Blending Mode to Multiply. You will now see the check.
Layer > Flatten Image
Name and save your design.

Checks to go!

14

It is advisable to check your pattern repeat to see how the design flows.
Edit > Define Pattern
Name your pattern and click OK. The pattern is saved in the pattern library.

Open a new document large enough to see your repeat pattern several times. You can change the size of your repeat pattern in the Image Size dialogue box. 50 x 50 cm (20 x 20 in) at 300dpi.
Edit > Fill > Pattern
Find your check in the Pattern Library.

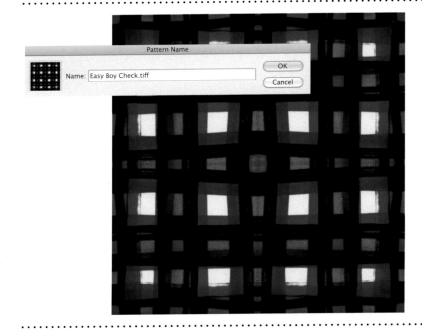

Pattern Name

Name: Easy Boy Check.tiff

OK
Cancel

15

Now that you know the process, you can easily create a series of Easy Boy Checks.

You are now ready to print your pattern. Details on how to do this are on pages 170-171.

HERE ARE SOME OTHER VERSIONS USING FINER FELT PEN MARKERS. EXPERIMENT!

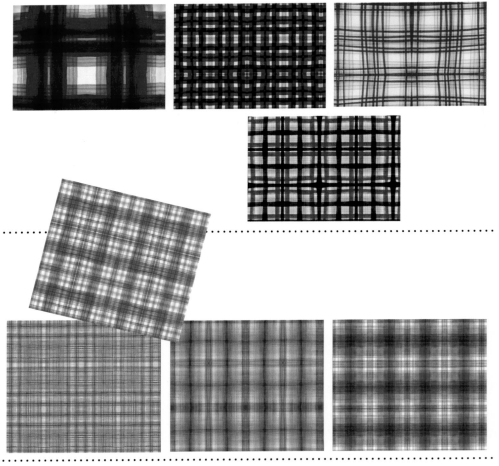

4
***

YOU WILL NEED

glue, black ink

tracing paper, pins

paintbrush, sellotape

newspapers, scissors

old magazines

masking tape

Vintage Floral Collage

Designer – Melanie Bowles

Have fun and create your own vintage collage arrangements using images from old books, photographs and patterned papers. Combining hand- and digital techniques, this tutorial shows you how to create a digitally collaged motif and put it into a half-drop pattern ready to repeat. Digitally print onto linen to give an added vintage texture and make it into a coat that is unique to you!

Getting Started

Visit your local charity shop to find glorious vintage gardening books and flower catalogues. You can also look through magazines for interesting papers and patterns. If you don't want to cut up an original book then make colour copies or scan in the pages.

Cut & paint

1

Scan the floral motifs you wish to use and print them out. Select and cut your floral images out.

To make strong silhouettes, place some tracing paper over the flowers you have selected to use and paint over the floral motifs with black ink.

Select & arrange

 2

Next, cut out your florals and tracings and arrange them on an A4 sheet of plain paper. For this design the idea is to keep the flowers as a group within the sheet. It is a good idea to photograph your arrangements now and record your compositions.

3

Choose some patterned and textured papers, in this case it is wood grain paper and a page of text from a vintage book.

Once you are happy with the arrangement, scan in your floral motifs, black silhouette tracings and patterned papers.

Remember to scan everything at 300dpi to keep the photographic details sharp. You now have your collage plan and you are ready to go!

ARTIST'S TIP

USE A NICE SOLID BLACK INK TO PAINT YOUR SHAPES SO THAT THEY SCAN WELL.

Digital collaging

Open your collage plan in Photoshop. Click on the Polygonal Lasso tool and draw roughly around the flower.
Edit > Copy the selection.

Open a new document.
File > New > Document A4-size at 300 dpi.
Edit > Paste

Your flower motif will appear. To remove the white surround, use the Magic Wand tool to select the white around the rose and delete.

Now continue to copy and paste your floral motifs to build up a grouping of flowers.
Select >All > Edit > Copy

ARTIST'S TIP
COMBINE BLACK AND WHITE AND COLOUR TO BUILD CONTRAST.

Pasting textures & patterns

 7

Now you will work with your black silhouettes to add some texture and pattern to the design.

Open your textured and patterned papers.

ARTIST'S TIP
ADD SPRIGS OF LEAVES TO ADD SHAPES AND INTEREST, IT'S LIKE FLOWER ARRANGING!

 8

Select the Magic Wand tool from the toolbar and select one of your silhouettes.
Edit > Copy
Paste the silhouette into your flower document.
Edit > Paste
Change the size of the silhouette if you wish.
Edit > Transform > Scale

 9

Open your texture document (in this case we used wood textured paper).
Select > All
Edit > Copy
Now open your flower document. From the toolbar choose the Magic Wand and select the black silhouette.
Edit > Paste Special > Paste Into

Your silhouette should now appear as wood textured.

Creating a half drop repeat

With your motif open
Select > All
Edit > Copy
Note the size of the design unit.
Image > Image Size
Jot down the pixel measurements. In this case it is 2080 x 2940 pixels.

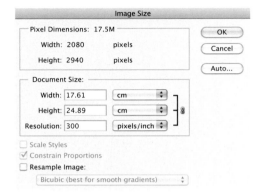

You will now divide the design unit into two.
Filter > Other > Offset
The Offset palette will appear. Ensure Wrap Around is selected.

Divide the vertical pixel by two and enter this in the Vertical box. Click OK. In this case it is 1470 pixels. Your image will be divided in two.
Image > Crop

To extend the canvas size:
Image > Canvas Size
Select the middle box on the left hand side. In Width, enter 200 percent.

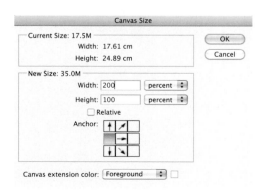

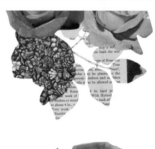

Changing the background

Remember you have already copied the original design unit.
Edit > Paste
Position the new motif next to the first.

Now Merge Visible your two layers. Remember, the background layer remains on its own so that you can change the colour if you wish. Your motif is now in a basic half drop repeat.

Turn the background layer on again. You can now try various colours on the background layer.
Edit > Fill > Foreground

Try different colours for different moods. If the design is for yourself then you may wish to change it to suit your own colouring, or even a pair of shoes that you are going to wear with it.

Offset filter

16

The Offset filter is one of the many filters in Photoshop. Here you can use the Offset filter to give more depth to your design.

17

Look at the repeat unit with the motif in the centre to see the negative space around it.
<u>Filter > Other > Offset</u>
Divide the Horizontal pixel measurement by four, in this case 1040 pixels.

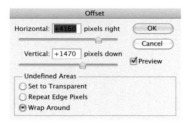

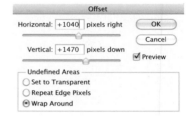

18

Now you can see the design in symmetry and the empty space around the motif.

You still have two layers, the design layer and the background layer.

Offset

 19

You can fill the new motifs with a tone of the background colour to give a subtle depth. Add new motifs and arrange in the space. Merge the layers but keep the background layer free.

ARTIST'S TIP
BY FILLING THIS SPACE THE DESIGN WILL HAVE A SENSE OF RHYTHM AND CONTINUITY WITHIN THE REPEAT.

 20

Again, offset the image to see the negative space.
Filter > Other > Offset

 21

Copy and paste some more black silhouette motifs into the space.

Defining your pattern

Add a page of text from the book by copying and pasting it into the motifs.

Merge Visible all the layers with motifs on. You can still adjust your background colour as it is still a layer on its own. When you are finished, flatten all layers.

Layer > Flatten Image

At this point you can change the scale of your repeat unit in the Image Size.

Your repeat unit is nearly ready to send off to the printers, but first check your repeat unit to see how the design flows.
To do this:

Edit > Define Pattern

Open a new document large enough to see the repeat several times.

Edit > Fill > Pattern

Scroll down in the Pattern Library to find your new pattern. Click OK.

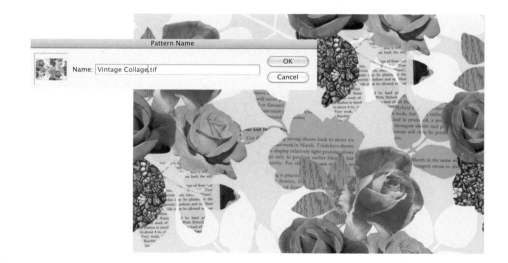

YOU ARE NOW READY TO PRINT YOUR PATTERN. DETAILS OF HOW TO DO THIS ARE ON PAGES 170-171.

5
***

Hackney Lights

Designer – Ruth Esmé Mitchell

Use the bokeh technique to create stunning out-of-focus photographs that will give depth and style to your printed designs. Bokeh creates soft blurred lights, perfect to translate into a soft overlaid pattern. Textile designer and photographer Ruth Esmé Mitchell photographed London city night lights, and used Photoshop to build a repeat pattern. Print it onto a luxury silk satin and make into a slouchy trouser ready to wear out.

Getting Started

Ruth Esmé Mitchell captures images on her travels around the world and from everyday life. Here she translates photographs from her journey through London to create her Hackney Lights print. You can document any journey, be inspired by the places around you.

Take your picture

Ruth uses a digital SLR camera to capture her night photography. With the focus on manual she uses the bokeh technique to take her shots. Bokeh is Japanese in origin and refers to blur or a blurry quality.

Take your picture

Bokeh is different from soft focus photography. In soft focus photography blurriness is added to the subject while the edges are retained in sharp focus, but with bokeh it is only an element of the image that is intentionally blurred. Bokeh is particularly effective at emphasizing certain points of light in the image.

Using a digital SLR camera with a 50 mm lens, open up your lens's aperture to its widest setting. Lenses with low F numbers like 2.8, 2.0, 1.8, 1.4 and lower are the best choices for bokeh shots. This large aperture ensures that you have a nice shallow depth of field.

Being close to your subject with a good distance between subject and background will help.

Take a series of varied photographs to experiment with this technique and you will achieve some stunning effects.

Cropping your photo

Use the USB cord to connect your camera to your computer, making sure the camera is turned on. Upload your photos from your camera to your computer.

Select and organise your pictures in your photo library.

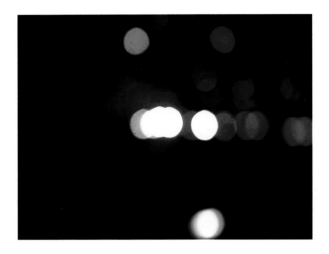

Select the Crop tool from the toolbar and make a selection ready to crop. Hit return to action the crop. This cropped image will now be made into the design.

Crop Tool

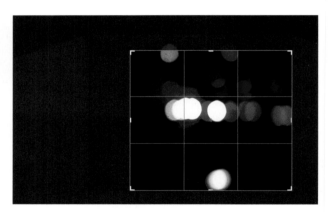

Before you start to build a pattern, spend a little time preparing your design by changing the scale and composing the image. To do this first flip your image 90 degrees.

Image > Image Rotation 90 CW

Copy your image

Select > All
Edit > Copy

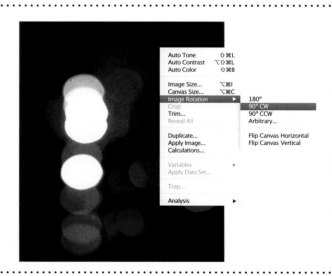

Building a pattern

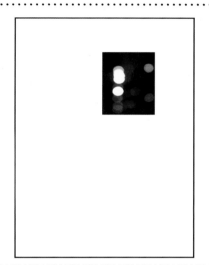

Open a new document sized 30 x 40 cm (12 x 16 in) at 300dpi
Edit > Paste
Now you need to reduce the size of the image and start to build up a pattern.
Select > All
Edit > Transform > Scale

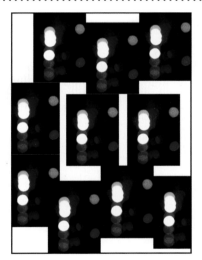

Continue to copy and paste your image to fill the canvas.

Compose the images to create a natural looking pattern.

With each image a new layer will be created which you can move around. Once you are happy with the arrangement, flatten your image.
Layer > Flatten Image

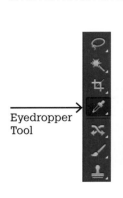

Eyedropper Tool

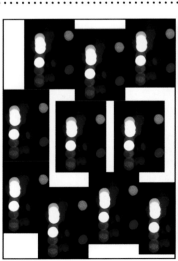

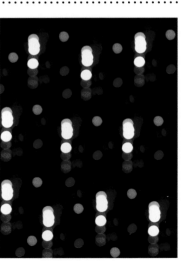

Now you are going to fill the white area. Select the Eyedropper tool from the toolbar.

Pick the dark background colour from one of the images to use as a fill. This colour becomes the foreground colour.

Select the Magic Wand, and with the Shift key held down select all the white areas.
Edit > Fill > Foreground Colour

Blending

Next you will give depth to the design.

Duplicate the layer by dragging it down to the New Layer icon at the bottom of the Layers palette. With the top layer selected, slightly shift it with the Move tool to reveal the layer below.

Now go to the Blending Mode at the top of the Layers palette. A drop down menu will appear. Choose Screen. This will reveal the layer below.

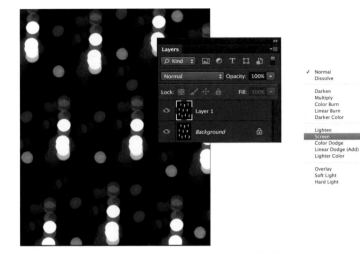

Now flip this layer in the opposite direction.
Edit Transform >
Flip Vertical
Flatten the two layers
Layer > Flatten Image

THE BASIC DESIGN IS COMPLETE!

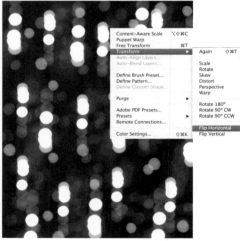

Begin to put the design into repeat using the Offset filter. Firstly remind yourself of the image size
Image > Image Size
In the document size put 50 percent in both Width and Height boxes. Jot down the pixel dimensions at the top of the dialogue box. In this case it is 1772 width x 2362 height.

Click Cancel to exit.

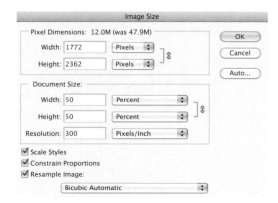

6

***

YOU WILL NEED

vintage books

needlepoint charts

1970s clothing

Bargello Dress

Designer – Melanie Bowles

Bargello stitch work is a needlepoint embroidery style which originated in Florence during the sixteenth century. The colourful, geometric design uses vertical stitches of many hues of one colour, which produces a stunning shading effect. Bargello had a revival in the 1970s. You will use digital techniques to create your very own Bargello design. Print your pattern onto a silk satin to create a stunning cocktail dress.

Getting Started

Look for vintage needlework books online or in thrift stores, where you may even discover garments or soft furnishings bearing Bargello designs from the 1970s.

Research

To begin with, spend some time researching the Bargello needlepoint technique.

Building a stitch

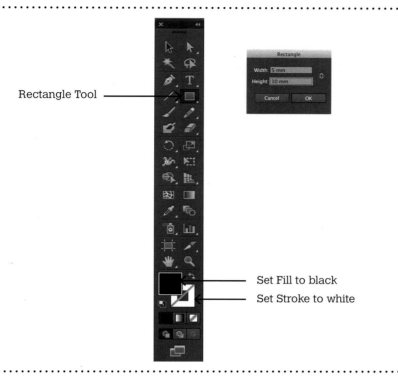

Rectangle Tool

Set Fill to black

Set Stroke to white

Open a new document in Illustrator sized 20cm x 50cm (7¾ x 19¾ in). Check the View menu to make sure Snap to Point is on.

View > Snap to Point

Set Fill to black and Stroke to none. To create your first stitch, select the Rectangle tool and double click on your document.

In the Rectangle dialogue box enter the measurements Width 5mm and Height 10mm and click OK.

Your first stitch will appear! Now you will duplicate the stitch vertically to build a column.

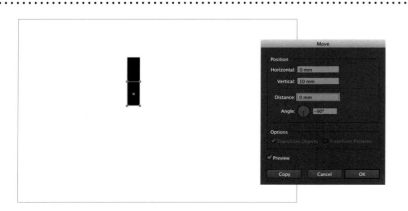

Select the rectangle with the Direct Selection tool. Hit Return. The Move dialogue box will appear. Enter the measurements:
Horizontal 0mm
Vertical 10mm

Click Copy in the dialogue box. A second stitch will appear beneath your first.

Building a stitch

5

Now duplicate this ten times to create a column of vertical stitches.

Use the shortcut keys on your computer: click
Command > D

6

Select your column of stitches
Edit > Copy > Paste
Edit > Paste
You now have two columns.

7

Next you are going to apply colour. Look at some of the images you researched to get ideas for blends.

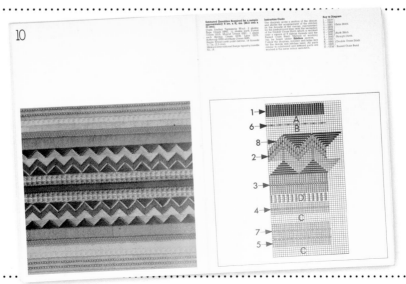

Now colour!

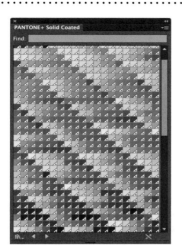

8

You can also use the Pantone Colour Book from your Swatch palette for blend ideas.

9

At the bottom left hand of your Swatch Palette you will see the Library icon; select and go to

Colour Books > PANTONE + Solid Coated

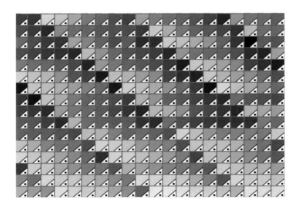

10

Here we used traditional Bargello combinations of blues and yellows.

Creating a blend

With your document open showing your two columns of stitches, select the top rectangle and select your colour from the Pantone Color Book.

Select the bottom rectangle and fill with white.

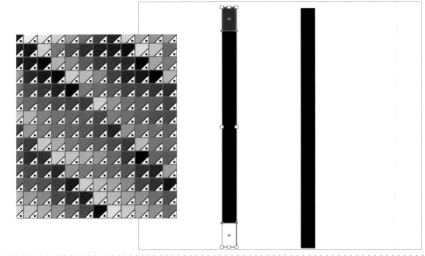

Select the Blend tool from the toolbar and double click.

The Blend Options dialogue box will appear. Choose the Specified Steps option and set to 10. Click OK.

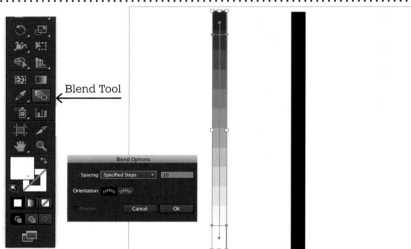

Blend Tool

Blend Options

Spacing: Specified Steps ▾ 10

Orientation:

Preview   Cancel   OK

Drag the Blend tool over the top rectangle to the bottom white rectangle. You will see your blend appear.

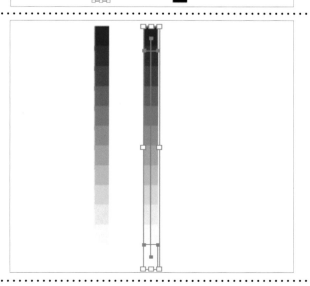

Reflecting colour

Repeat this process with your other column of stitches. Select the yellow column and drag to the side as you will work on the blue one first.

Reflect Tool

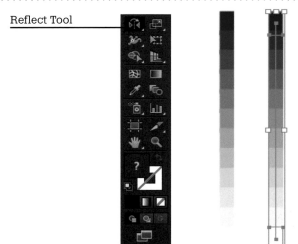

Select your first column
Edit > Copy > Paste
With the copy still selected go to the toolbar and select the Reflect tool.

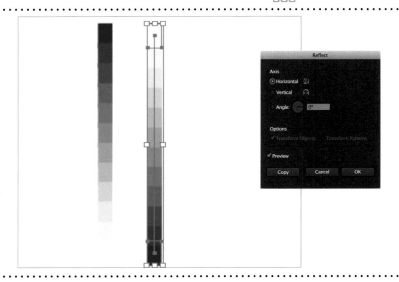

In the Reflect dialogue box choose to reflect the Horizontal.

Creating a chevron

17

Now it's time to create the chevron pattern which is a distinctive feature in many Bargello designs.

Select the column with the Direct Selection tool and move the second column to the top of the first column so it Snaps to Point.

Repeat the process with your second colour column.

Direct Selection Tool

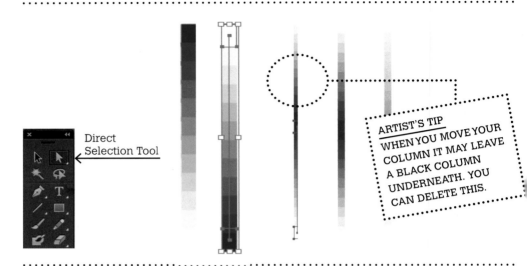

ARTIST'S TIP
WHEN YOU MOVE YOUR COLUMN IT MAY LEAVE A BLACK COLUMN UNDERNEATH. YOU CAN DELETE THIS.

18

Select the yellow column with the Selection tool. Move it to Snap to Point with the bottom of the first column.

Check they are accurately aligned
View > Outline
Go back to preview
View > Preview

To group the two columns together
Select > All
Object >Group

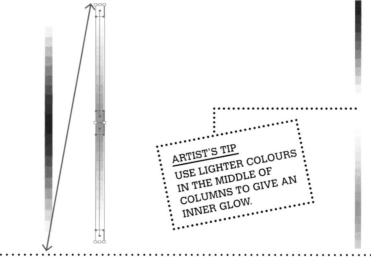

ARTIST'S TIP
USE LIGHTER COLOURS IN THE MIDDLE OF COLUMNS TO GIVE AN INNER GLOW.

19

Now create a chevron. With your column selected hit Return The Move dialogue box will appear.

Enter the measurements
Horizontal 5mm
Vertical 10mm
Distance 0

The Angle will set itself once you have put in these measurements. Click Copy.

Duplicate this action ten times to create the first half of the chevron.

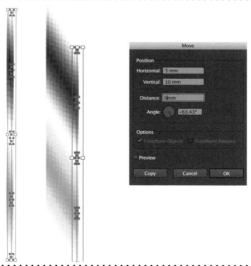

Building pattern

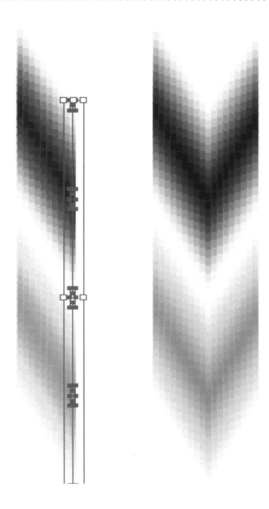

20

Select the last column and the Direct Selection tool. Hit Return. In the Move dialogue box enter the measurements
Horizontal 5 mm
Vertical -10 mm
Distance 0

The Angle will set itself once you have put in these measurements.
Click Copy.

Duplicate this action nine times to create the second half of the chevron. Use the shortcut key
Command > D

You have made the basic chevron motif for your Bargello design.

Move this bottom point to the top of the first column

21

To group all the columns together to create one unit
Select > All
Object > Group
In the View menu click on
Outline View > Outline
Edit > Copy
Edit > Paste

Preparing for repeat

22

With your copied chevron motif open, from the toolbar use the Direct Selection tool and select the bottom tip of your copied chevron. Move this to fit into place at the top of the first chevron so it slots into place.

In the Edit menu, copy the section again and drag the unit to the bottom of the first chevron.

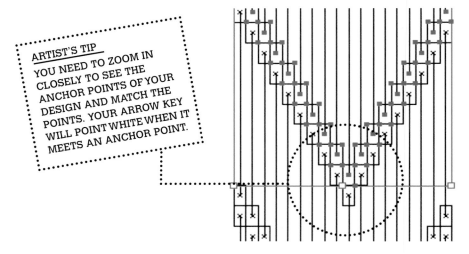

ARTIST'S TIP
YOU NEED TO ZOOM IN CLOSELY TO SEE THE ANCHOR POINTS OF YOUR DESIGN AND MATCH THE POINTS. YOUR ARROW KEY WILL POINT WHITE WHEN IT MEETS AN ANCHOR POINT.

23

Your image will go beyond the document box. Next you will find the repeat unit and crop it.

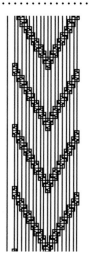
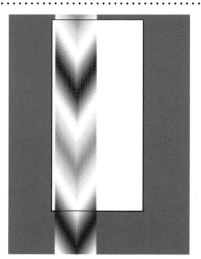

24

To crop the repeat unit, you first need to prepare an area of your chevron motif to crop. Go to
View > Rulers > Show Rulers
You are going to place rulers to the top and the bottom of the repeat unit.

Zoom in and choose a top point of the design and drag the ruler to that point. Now find the same point further down the design.

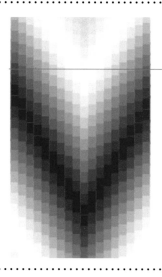

Cropping the unit

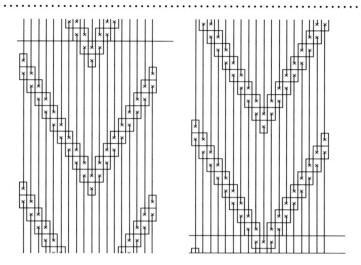

25

In the View menu click on Outline.

Check the rulers are correctly placed.

In View click on Preview to go back to the coloured artwork.

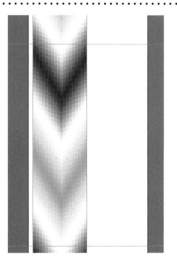

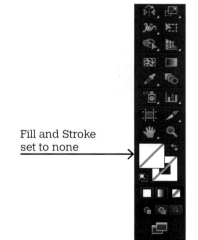

Fill and Stroke set to none →

26

Drag the horizontal rulers to the edge of the design, check in Outline mode that they are correctly positioned.

Select the Marquee tool. Set the Fill and Stroke boxes to none. Draw a box from the top ruler to the bottom ruler. This is a boundary box that will crop the chevron.

Path ▶
Pattern ▶
Blend ▶
Envelope Distort ▶
Perspective ▶
Live Paint ▶
Image Trace ▶
Text Wrap ▶
Clipping Mask ▶ Make ⌘7
Compound Path ▶ Release ⌥⌘7
Artboards ▶ Edit Mask
Graph ▶

27

Select your boundary box and the chevron.
Select > Select All

In the Object menu scroll down and select Clipping Mask then click on Make. This will crop your design so it is now in a clean repeat.

Save and name your repeat unit.

Colourways

Have fun with the colours now.

Select the Magic Wand tool and carefully select one of the rectangles.

Choose a colour from the Swatches palette and it will change the whole blend!

When you have decided on your colourway select the Direct Selection tool and your repeat unit
Edit > Copy

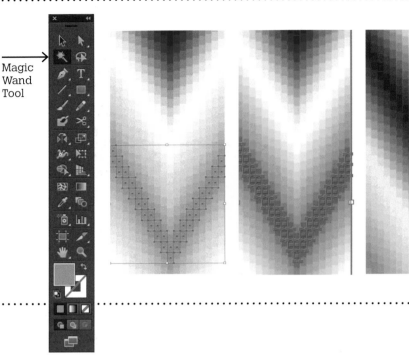

Magic
Wand
Tool

Name and save your design. Now you will export it to Photoshop. Scroll down to Export, and in the dialogue box choose location, name, and format as TIFF.

A TIFF dialogue box will appear. Set Colour Mode to RGB and resolution to 300dpi.

Click OK.

Open Photoshop, locate your chevron design and
File > Open
Now test it out as a repeat
Edit > Define Pattern
Name the pattern and click OK.

Open a new document 40 x 60cm (16 x 24 in) at 300dpi
Edit > Fill > Pattern
Now you can see the full, final chevron effect.

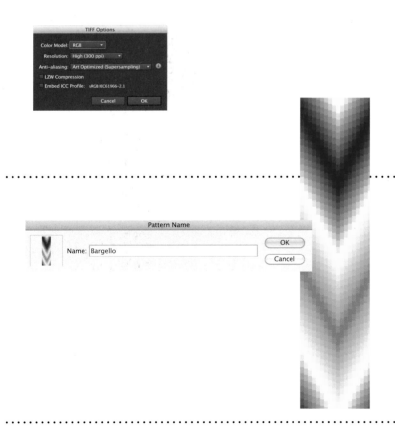

7
***

YOU WILL NEED

digital camera

seed packets

gardening magazines

Dahlia skirt

Designer – Melanie Bowles

Flowers have always been a traditional motif in textile design. With digital printing you can now use your own photographs and images from magazines or books to create glorious, hyper-real floral designs. This tutorial shows you how to select flowers from photographs, compose and arrange them to make a stunning repeat pattern. Print onto a cotton sateen and make into a beautiful special-occasion skirt that will make heads turn.

Getting Started

Head down to an allotment in autumn to find glorious dahlias in full bloom, or buy a bunch from your local florist and take photographs of a range of flower heads. You can also collect images from seed packets or magazines to make wonderful floral designs.

Dahlia
Dwarf Border Mixed

brought to
you by **B&Q**

£1.28
€1.45

My dahlia photos

 1

With a good digital camera, take some close-up photographs in different colours, from different angles. You will be using about ten flower heads. Connect your camera to your computer. Make sure the camera is turned on. Go to My Computer, find the icon for the camera (after it is plugged in) and drag the pictures to another folder.

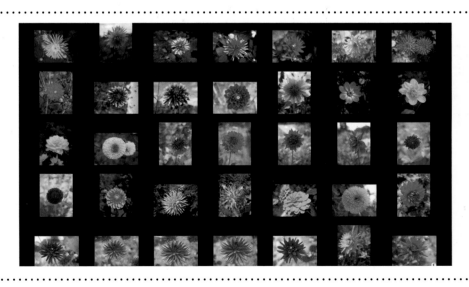

Choose your floral

Open one of your dahlia photos in Photoshop.

Change the image resolution to 300dpi.
> **Image > Image Size > 300dpi**

It's important to adjust the size to 300dpi to maintain a sharp image.

Select an individual flower from its background. There are several selection tools you can use but the Pen tool will allow an accurate and sensitive selection.

When using the Pen tool a path will be created which can be saved and edited at any time. A digital stylus will make the job quicker and easier as it simulates a pen, but if you don't have one a mouse will work just as well.

ARTIST'S TIP
DON'T RUSH THE NEXT STAGES, AS THEY WILL TAKE TIME AND CONCENTRATION!

Pen tool

Select the Pen tool from the toolbar. In the Paths palette, click on the Create New Path icon. A new path will appear.

In the Option bar select the Path and Exclude Overlapping Shapes icons.

Path

Exclude Overlapping Shapes

Create New Path

Zoom in to the image and click around the edges of the flower. Anchor points will appear that you can edit and add curves after you have drawn around it.

Once you have drawn around the edge of your flower you can refine it using the Direct Selection tool. This will let you move a single anchor point and allows you to retouch any anchor points that you are not happy with.

Paths

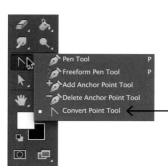

Convert Point Tool

You can edit your anchor points and create a curve with the Convert Point tool. This can take a bit of practise but it's worth it to create a smooth curve.

Zoom in to the area where you want to create a curve. Click on the anchor point you want to curve with the Convert Point tool. When you pull the anchor point a line called the tangent line will appear. The tangent line controls the curvature of the curve. Pull on one of the tangent lines and drag and that path will bend.

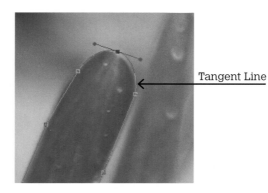

Tangent Line

8

As you draw you will see your paths being created in the Paths palette. This is making an outline around the flower.

Selection

In the Paths palette you can see the path you have just created. Save the path using the Paths drop down menu. Make sure the path you have just created is active by clicking on it in the Paths palette to highlight it. Once you are happy with your path click on the Load Selection icon at the bottom of the Paths palette to make your path into a live selection.

Load Selection

When you are happy with your flower image, you should refine your selection
Select > Refine Edge
Now change the Feather slider to soften the edge of your selection.

Click OK when you are satisfied.

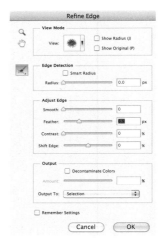

Now you are ready to copy and paste your selection onto a new document.
Edit > Copy

Arrange

Open a new document sized 20 x 20 cm (7¾ x 7¾ in) at 300dpi in RGB
Edit > Paste
Place your flower in the centre of the document.
Edit > Transform > Scale
Scale your flower to sit nicely in the centre.

Now go back to your original photograph and use the Pen tool to select different flower heads.

Remember to save the path you create. You can see all of the paths you have created in the Paths palette.

Continue to select flowers as before and copy and paste them into your document, arranging them in each corner and scaling them to fit. Working with the Layers palette can be confusing, so the next stage will guide you through how to manage your layers.

Now that you have selected your flower heads you will notice in the Layers palette that you have several layers. Turn the Background layer off and Merge Visible Layer. You should now have two layers: the background layer and the design layer. With the top layer selected
Select > All
Edit > Copy

Building a repeat

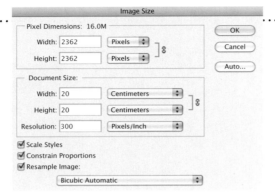

Go to
Image > Image Size
Under Pixel Dimensions jot down the pixel size of your image In this case it is 2362 x 2362 pixels.

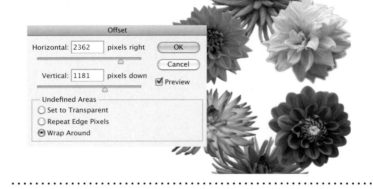

With the top layer selected go to
Filters > Other > Offset
Divide the Vertical measurement by two to 1181. Ensure that Wrap Around is selected in the Offset dialogue box.

This will cut your image in half but repeat it on the outside.

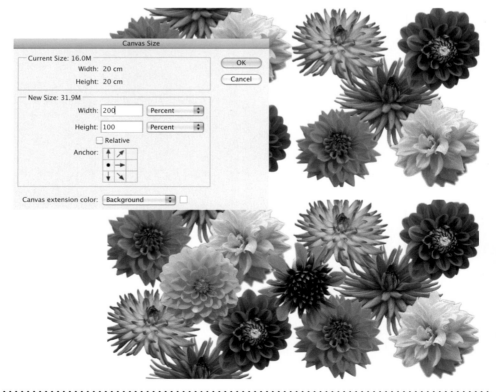

You will now extend the canvas size.
Image > Canvas Size
Click on the left hand middle box of the Anchor grid and change the Width to 200 percent.

Place two new flowers in the centre gaps and scale to fit.

Turn the Background layer off and Merge Visible Layers in the centre gaps.

You will now extend the canvas size.
Image > Canvas Size
Select the left hand middle box and change the Width to 200 percent.

Place two new flowers in the centre gaps.

Your all-over floral!

 18

Offset the image by dividing both Horizontal and Vertical by half and continue to fill in the centre gaps.

 19

Fill in your new gaps with two new flowers.

Turn the Background layer off and Merge Visible Layers.

 20

Nearly there!

You will now use the Offset Filter for the last time, moving the sliders vertically and horizontally to show the empty gaps.

 21

Fill in the gaps with two new flowers. Turn the Background layer off and Merge Visible Layers.

You have finished!

Blur filter

22

The Background layer is still free to add a colour. Fill with black before you flatten the whole image. Once you are happy with the result
Layer > Flatten Image
The repeat unit is now done!

23

You can apply any filter or effects you want. Here the Blur filter was used to soften the images.
Filter > Blur > Smart Blur
Move the slider for the desired effect.

Note: the filters will only work in RGB mode.

24

You can change the size of your repeat unit if you wish. It's good to do a paper printout to see the real scale. Once you are happy test your pattern repeat by filling into a new document
Edit > Define Pattern
Name your pattern.
This repeat unit is 40 x 20 cm (15¾ x 1¾ in). To test the repeat create a new document 80cm x 40cm (31½ x 15¾ in)
Select Edit > Fill
Select Pattern and find your design unit under Custom Pattern. Check your repeat for any breaks in seams.

YOUR REPEAT UNIT IS NOW READY TO SEND OFF TO THE PRINTERS!

8

* * *

YOU WILL NEED

scrap and vintage
fabrics, scissors
patchwork patterns

Clara's Patchwork

Designer – Clara Vuletich

Designer, researcher and yoga teacher Clara Vuletich reinvents the traditional craft of patchwork, combining colours, pattern and narratives. Using favourite scraps and vintage fabrics, this tutorial shows how to create a digital patchwork. Digitally print onto a soft needlecord and make into a comfortable A-line skirt.

Getting Started

Collect, buy or borrow scraps of fabrics. Research traditional patchwork designs, whether in vintage books or online. You'll find inspiration to create your own unique digital patchwork.

Planning

Clara begins by collecting a variety of fabrics to create her personal patchwork story. These can include vintage fabrics that evoke special memories.

Planning

Put your found fabrics together in groups of colours to see how the patterns interact with each other. This tutorial uses a combination of checks, plaids, stripes and florals with some block colour.

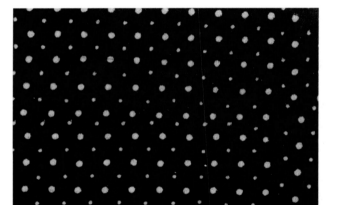

Scan in your fabrics at 300dpi on an A4 scanner. Open Photoshop and save in a folder named Patchwork.

Experiment with traditional patchwork. Look through some patchwork books for different layouts and patterns, or research the internet for patchwork pattern ideas.

Designing

There are numerous ways to create patchwork designs. This design is based on a simple triangle pattern called 'Birds in the Air'.

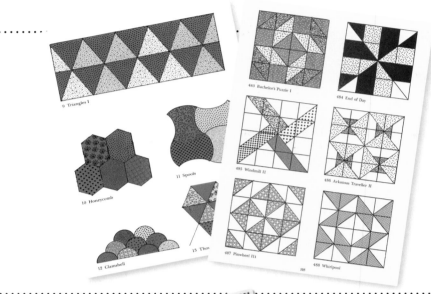

Plan your patchwork by hand first and play with some paper combinations.

Print your scanned patterns out on paper.

Cut out squares of 8 x 8 cm (3 x 3 in) and cut them in half to make triangles. Play around with the squares to make different arrangements, securing them with tape.

Once you have a plan you can start to create your digital patchwork. Remember, this is a lot quicker than sewing it!

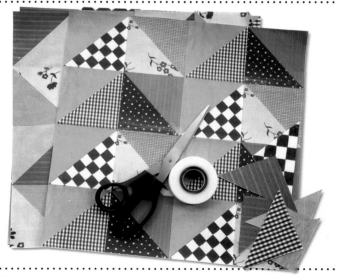

Preparing patchwork

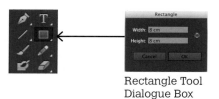

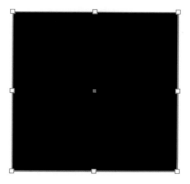

Rectangle Tool
Dialogue Box

Open a new A4 document in Illustrator. Make sure Snap to Point is on.
View > Snap to Point
Use the Rectangle tool to create an 8 x 8 cm (3 x 3 in) square. Double click on the Rectangle tool and the Rectangle dialogue box will appear. Input 8 x 8cm (3 x 3 in). Click OK. A square will appear. Select the square, open the Edit menu and select Fill. In the Fill dialogue box, select Black.

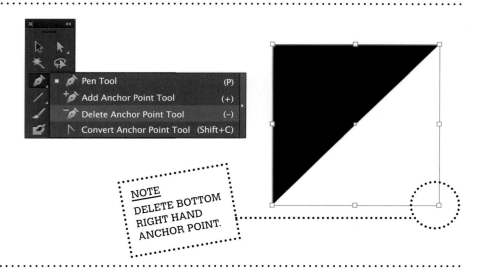

NOTE
DELETE BOTTOM RIGHT HAND ANCHOR POINT.

With your square selected Go to the toolbar and select the small arrow on the bottom right of the Pen tool. A drop down menu will appear. Choose the Delete Anchor Point tool and, with this selected, click on the bottom right hand anchor point of your square. It will delete this anchor point and create a white triangle shape.

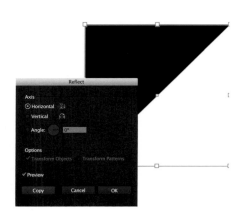

Now you can create a new triangle by using the Transform tools. With your triangle selected go to
Object > Transform > Reflect
A dialogue box will appear. Select Horizontal and click Copy. A new triangle will appear that has been reflected.

Making a patch unit

To build up a basic patch unit you're going to vertically reflect the second triangle. Go to
Object > Transform > Reflect
A dialogue box will appear. Select Vertical, click OK.

Your second triangle will be reflected, so you will now have two triangles to make your first patch.

Select the bottom right hand triangle, open the Edit menu and select Fill. In the Fill dialogue box, select a colour.

Fill this triangle with a colour. Group both triangles together.

Choose Object in the Option menu.
Object > Group

With square selected go to
Object > Transform > Reflect
The Reflect dialogue box will appear. Select Vertical and click Copy.

Using the Direct Select tool, select the top left corner anchor point and snap it to place to the other square's top right corner anchor point. When the Direct Select arrow goes white it has snapped to the other anchor point.

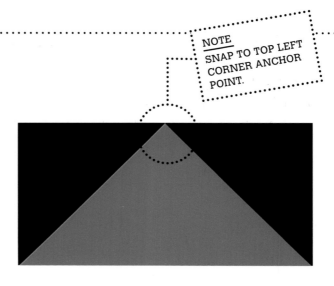

NOTE
SNAP TO TOP LEFT CORNER ANCHOR POINT.

Basic patch unit

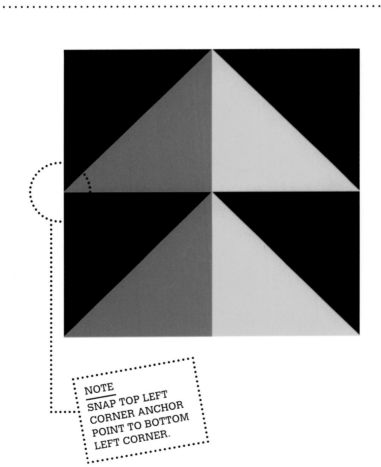

14

Select the new bottom left hand triangle in the square and fill with a new colour: open the Edit menu and select Fill. In the Fill dialogue box, select a new colour.

Group together your two squares. Go to
Object > Group

15

Select your two-square unit. In the Option menu choose
Edit > Copy
Select Edit > Paste
From the toolbar choose the Direct Selection tool and select the copied unit at the top left corner. Move it to Snap to Point to the first unit's lower left hand corner.

Select both units. Go to
Object > Group
Your eight-triangle unit is now ready to copy to Photoshop.

Select your unit and copy. In the Option menu select
Edit > Copy

NOTE
SNAP TOP LEFT CORNER ANCHOR POINT TO BOTTOM LEFT CORNER.

Paste in patterns

16

Open Photoshop and create a new document 16cm x 16cm (6¼ x 6¼ in). Go to the View menu and check Snap To All is on.
View > Snap to All
In the Options menu select
Edit > Paste
A Paste dialogue box will appear. Select Pixels and click OK. The copied unit will be pasted into your new document. Hit Return to place it.

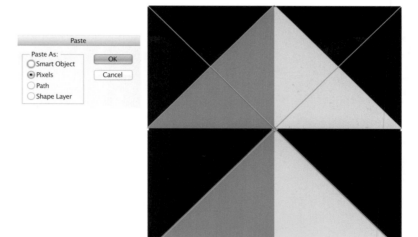

17

In Photoshop open your folder of scanned fabrics, select and open one. Go to
Select > All
Edit > Copy
Go back to the Patchwork unit. Select the Magic Wand and the top left triangle of your patchwork unit. Paste the fabric into the unit. Your first triangle is selected. In the Option menu select
Edit > Paste Special > Paste Into

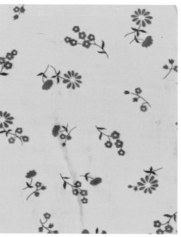

18

Your fabric will be pasted into the selected triangle. You will see a new layer appear in the Layers palette. Select the Move tool. You can move the fabric around until you are happy with the placement. Now you are ready to paste another fabric in.

In the Layers palette select the layer with the patchwork unit on, in this case Layer 1.

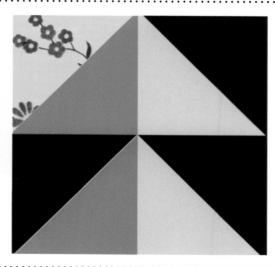

Making patchwork

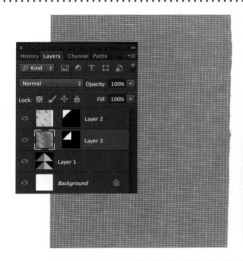
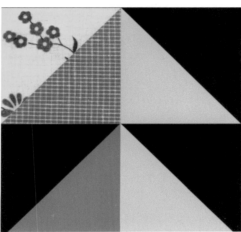

 19

Open a new fabric, go to
Select > All
Edit > Copy
Now back to the patchwork.
Use the Magic Wand to
select the next triangle. In
the Option menu choose
Edit > Paste Special >
Paste Into
Your fabric will be pasted
into the second triangle.
In the Layers palette a new
layer will appear. Continue
until your unit is complete.

 20

Remember to go back to
the original patchwork
layer (Layer 1) every time
you select a new triangle.
With your patchwork
complete you should have
10 layers.
Layers > Flatten Layers
You will now create a half
drop repeat. (If you want to
just have your Patchwork
unit as a simple block
repeat, then your design is
ready to print!)

 21

In the Options menu select
your patchwork unit.
Select > All
Put a centrepoint in the
design as a guide for the
half drop.
Edit > Free Transform
Crosshairs will appear in the
centre. In the View menu go
to the rulers at the top of
the document window and
pull down until it snaps into
place over the crosshairs.
Click Escape.

Creating a repeat

22

Select your patchwork unit and copy it
Edit > Copy

Now extend the canvas horizontally.
Image > Canvas Size
Select the middle left hand square in the Anchor Grid. In Width put 200 percent. Hit Return.

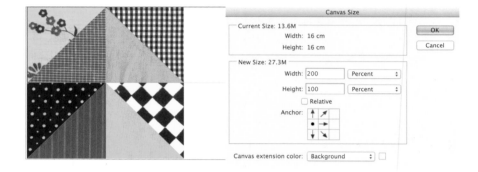

23

Edit > Paste
Now move the pasted unit to the bottom so the top snaps to the ruler.

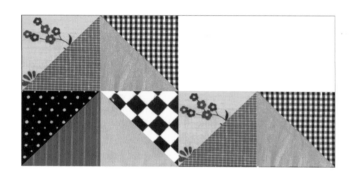

24

Duplicate the new pasted layer.
Edit > Paste
Move the pasted unit so the bottom snaps to the top of the ruler. Flatten the layers.
Layer > Flatten Image

Your design is now in a half drop repeat and ready to send to the printers.
To check the layout
Edit > Select All
Edit > Define Pattern
Open a new document 64 x 64cm (25 x 25 in) Fill your new document with the new pattern
Edit > Fill > Pattern

Find your pattern in the Pattern Library and click OK. You can now see how your pattern repeats.

9
***

Digital Shibori

Designer – Joanna Fowles

Sydney-based textile designer Joanna Fowles is a printer, dyer and digital crafter. Joanna is passionate about the art of Shibori, a traditional Japanese form of textile dyeing. In this tutorial she shows how to transform a swatch of Shibori into a stunning digital pattern that keeps the character of the craft. Digitally print it onto a silk/cotton mix and make into an easywear dress.

Getting Started

Firstly, have some fun with dyeing. Get some ideas by researching Shibori dye techniques and, using a domestic dye, wrap, fold and tie your fabric. Scan in and create some stunning designs in Photoshop.

The technique

1

Shibori is the Japanese term for tie-dye, stitch-dye, fold-dye and pole-wrap-dye techniques which create pattern by resist methods of dyeing. There is always an element of surprise in making Shibori, which contributes to its special appeal. Traditionally the natural dye Indigo was used, but here Joanna uses an easy domestic blue dye to create a similar effect.

Dyeing

 2

For this tutorial Joanna used a pole-wrap technique to build up sample pieces of dyed cloth. Start by wrapping a piece of cotton or silk around a plastic pole such as a short length of drainpipe. Next, bind the cloth with string.

Prepare the domestic dye in a bucket or basin. It is advisable to wear strong rubber gloves. Follow the instructions on the dye packet to mix your dye. When the dye solution is ready, immerse the pole into the dye.

 3

There are several ways to achieve resist patterns, by using clothes pegs, knotting and stitching on the cloth or by using different thicknesses of string to wrap the cloth. Be willing to experiment, wear rubber gloves and have fun!

Pattern

4

After the dyeing process unwrap the fabric to reveal the surprise pattern inside!

5

To produce a large enough piece of fabric to make a dress would be very difficult. By creating Shibori samples that can be built into a repeat in Photoshop and digitally printing the fabric is a perfect way to make a Shibori dress.

Produce various samples and select the ones you want to work with further on the computer.

6

Once you have a selection you are ready to scan in one of your Shibori fabrics.

Scanning & cropping

Scan in your Shibori fabric at 300dpi. Your image needs to be RGB.

Crop Tool

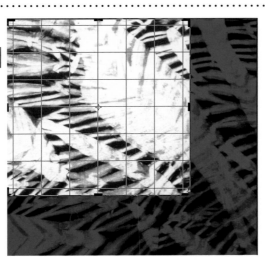

You can work with the whole scanned fabric or crop a section.

Select the Crop tool. In the Crop tool option bar select the 1x1 square option, and a grid will appear around the design. Pull the corner arrows to reduce the crop selection, and move around to select which part of the design you wish to use. Hit Return.

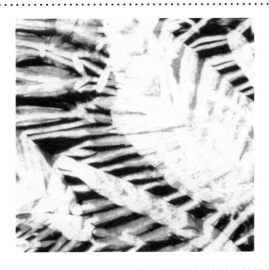

Now you have a selected area to build a Shibori repeat pattern with.
You will use a reflection technique to build the design, which echoes the original method of Shibori fold-dye.

Select your design
Select > All
Edit > Copy

Building a design

10

To extend the canvas size
Image > Canvas Size
A dialogue box will pop up.
Select the middle left square
of the Anchor grid. Set the
width to 200 percent so
that the canvas doubles in
width. Click OK.

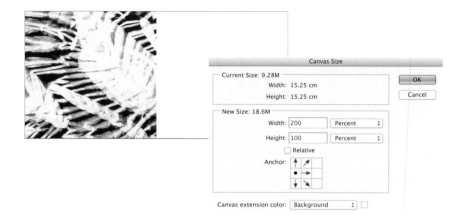

11

In step nine the original
cropped image was copied.
Now you can paste it into
the new canvas size.
Edit > Paste
Move the image so it clicks
into place in the empty
space. To mirror the new
pasted image
Edit > Transform
Scroll down and select Flip
Horizontal. Your image will
now be mirrored.

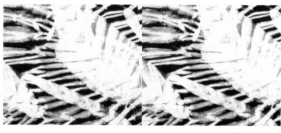

12

In the Layers palette you
will have two layers that
need to be flattened
Image > Flatten Image
Copy your new unit
Select > All
Edit > Copy

Reflect

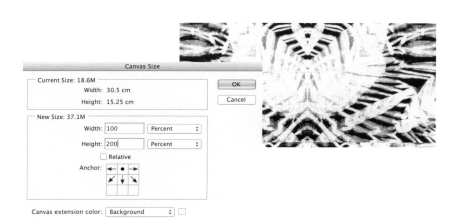

Once again you are going to extend the canvas size, this time the height.
Image > Canvas Size
Select the top middle square and set the width to 200 percent so the canvas doubles in height.

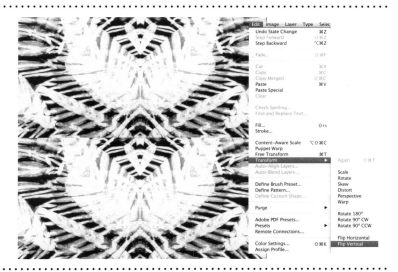

Edit > Paste
Paste your copied unit into the new space, move it so it is in place.
Flip it Vertically
Edit > Transform > Flip Vertically.

Flatten your two layers
Image > Flatten Image

You now have a perfect mirrored design unit!

Blends

The Shibori process always has a lovely element of surprise, which makes the technique so appealing. Now the digital process gets really exciting! You are going to use Blending tools, which introduce their own element of the unexpected with some surprising results.

In the Layers palette, first duplicate the layer by dragging it to the Duplicate Layer icon along the bottom of the palette box.

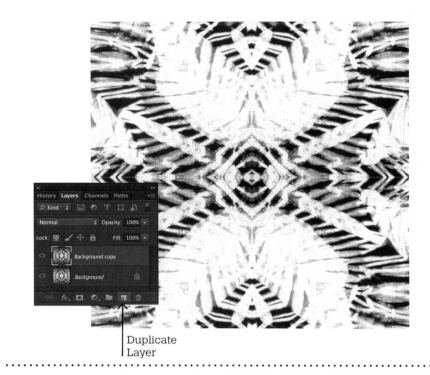

Duplicate
Layer

Now rotate the new layer.
Edit > Transform
Scroll down and select 90 degrees CW.

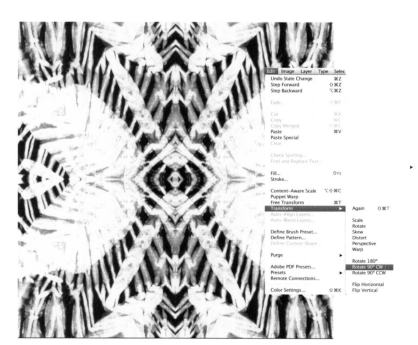

Colour & repeat

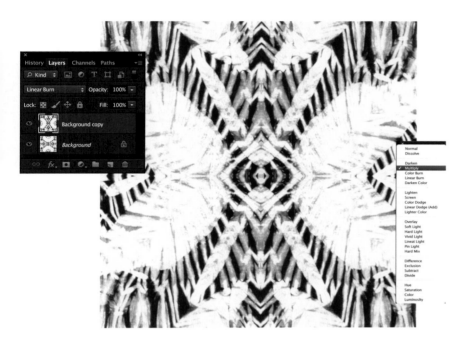

 18

Now to add some effects. In the top right corner of the Layers palette in the Blending Mode palette, click on the arrow in the drop down menu to view the blending options. Experiment with the options to create different effects.

 19

Amazing effects can be achieved with the Blend Mode, adding to the magic of Shibori.

Tie-dye effects

To add another colour to create a tie-dye look, alter the colour of the top layer. Select the top layer.
Image > Adjustments Hue/Saturation
Move the Hue Slider to change the colour.

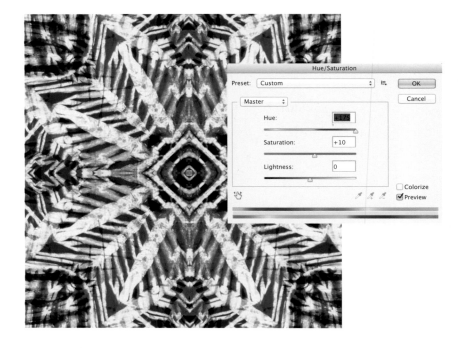

For this tutorial, we stay true to the Indigo dye colour of traditional Shibori. Flatten your image and test out your repeat.
Image > Flatten Image
Select > All
Edit > Define Pattern
Name your pattern and press OK. Open a new document four times the size to test your pattern.
Edit > Fill > Select Pattern
and find your digital Shibori pattern in the Pattern Library.

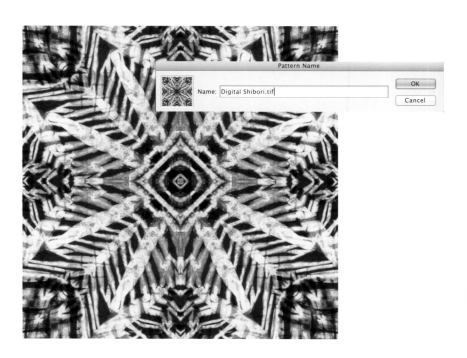

10

***

YOU WILL NEED

your favourite
colouring book
a friend, scissors
glue, felt tip pens

Colour Me In

Designer – Nina Chakrabarti

Have some friends around to colour in!
Choose your favourite colouring book
and just start colouring in motifs with
felt tip pens. Cut and arrange your motifs
into endless patterns ready to put into
a simple Photoshop block repeat. Print
onto a cotton poplin and make into fun
PJ bottoms.

Getting Started

You can use any colouring book that has interesting repeat motifs. Inspired by nail art, we used *My Wonderful World of Fashion* by Nina Chakrabarti. Simply colour the drawings with felt tip pens, cut them out and arrange in patterns.

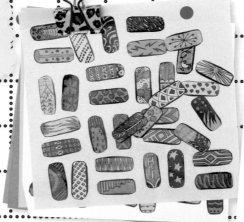

Choose a book

 1

Start by choosing your favourite colouring book. For this tutorial we selected The Nail Art Gallery from *My Wonderful World of Fashion*.

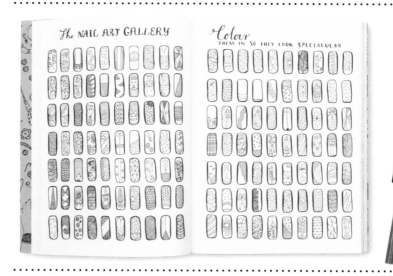

Planning

Colour in the nail art drawings with felt tip pens. Have fun, and use a combination of bright colours.

Next, cut out your coloured-in nails and arrange them on some coloured paper. You can use origami paper.

ARTIST'S TIP
STICK SOME DOUBLE-SIDED TAPE ON THE BACK OF YOUR CUT NAILS SO YOU CAN REARRANGE THEM INTO DIFFERENT LAYOUTS AND COMBINATIONS.

Crop
& offset

Once you are happy with
your arrangement, scan
in your design at 300dpi.
Open Photoshop and
save your scan in a folder
named Colour Me In.

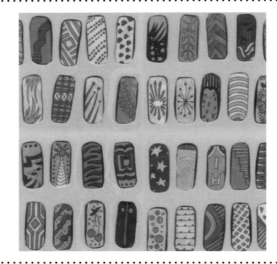

Open your nail art design
in Photoshop. Click on the
Crop tool icon from the
toolbar. Move the corner
anchor points around the
area of the design you want
to crop. Click OK.

Crop
Tool

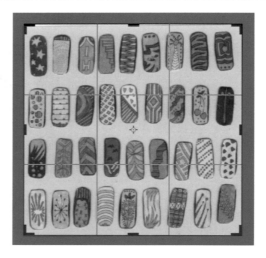

You will put the design into
a simple block repeat, but
first check the seams.
   Filter > Other > Offset
The Offset dialogue box
will appear. Move both the
Horizontal and Vertical
sliders to reveal the seam.
Ensure that Wrap Around
in the Offset dialogue box
is selected.

Mend & move

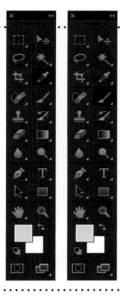

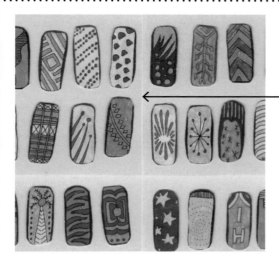

Mend these faint seams

Here you can see a slight seam that needs mending. Select the Eyedropper tool from the toolbar for colour-matching. Hover it over the seam to pick the background colour of the design. Now select the Paintbrush tool and paint over the seam.

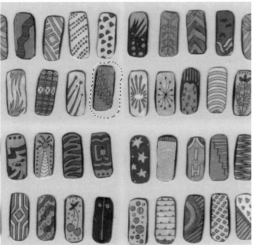

Lasso Tool

Move Tool

Switch Foreground to Background colour

Now move some of the nails so that they look more evenly distributed. In the tool panel switch the Foreground colour to the Background colour.

Select the Lasso tool from the toolbar. Draw around the nail you want to move, and with the Move tool adjust the nail into the position you want.

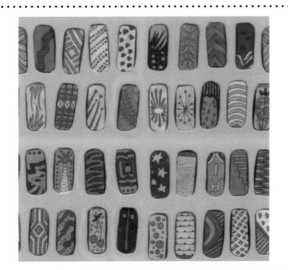

With all the nails nicely distributed and the design in repeat, you can add some more pattern.

Paint & colour

Select the Eyedropper tool from the toolbar and select colour from part of your design.

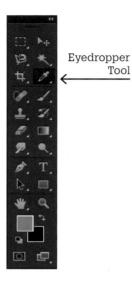

Eyedropper Tool

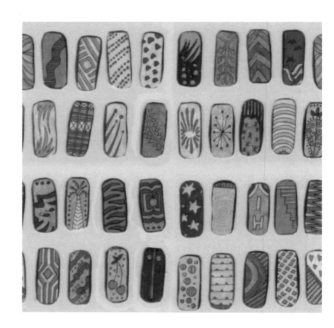

Select a Brush tool and the Brush tool option bar will appear. In the option bar choose a brush and size. Paint directly onto your design to add some dots. To create your own custom brush see page 14. Continue until you are happy with the added pattern.

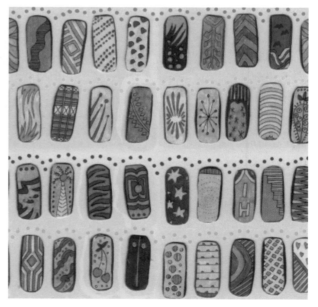

Colour adjustment

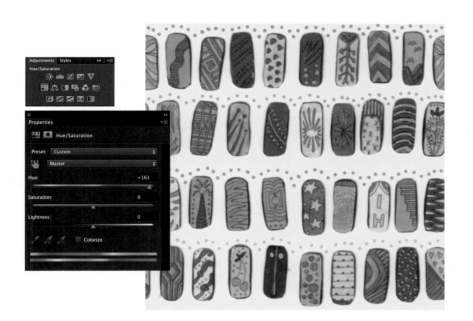

12

You can still play with the colour of your design by changing the Hue and Saturation.

In the Window menu, click on Adjustment. A dialogue box will appear, click on the Hue/Saturation icon and a slider bar will appear. Move the slider to change the colours in your design. A new layer will be created, which will protect your original artwork.

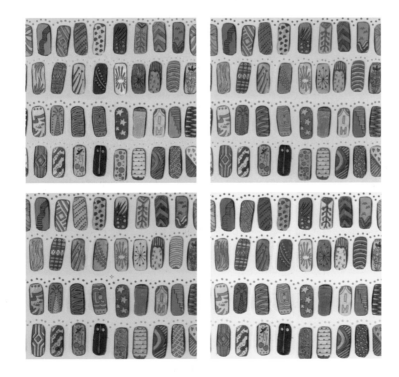

13

Play with some alternative colourways. Once you are happy with your design, flatten the artwork. With your design layer highlighted, click on the menu button in the top right hand corner of the Layers palette and a drop down menu will appear.

Layer > Flatten Image

Pattern
fill

Your design is now in repeat and ready to send off to the printers. At this point you can change the size of your pattern

Image > Image Size

Change the unit of measurement to percent and adjust as required. Now test your new pattern

Edit > Define Pattern

Open a new document four times larger than your design and fill with your pattern

Edit > Fill

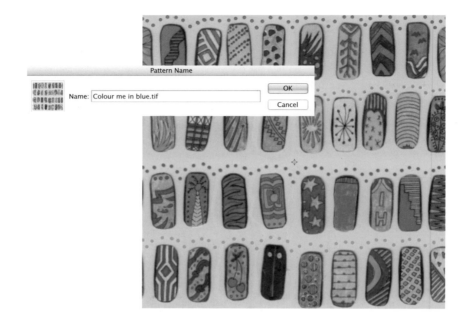

Click on Custom Pattern to reveal the patterns stored in the Pattern Library. Locate your pattern.

For this design we made a little star paint brush motif from the Brush panel in Photoshop, which allows you to create your own custom brush from almost any motif, and then paint freely with it.

**HAVE FUN
EXPERIMENTING
WITH A RANGE OF
DESIGNS!**

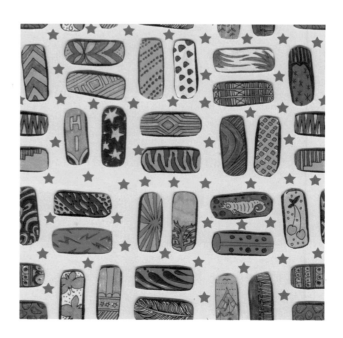

11
***

YOU WILL NEED

digital camera to take photos of buildings or reference images

Monotone Man

Designer – Henry Muller

This is a simple tutorial so you can experiment with several photographs to create striking pattern formations that can be put into an easy mirror repeat using basic techniques in Photoshop. Use tough canvas cotton to make up a moody, monotone bomber jacket.

Getting Started

Urban buildings create strong geometric shapes which provide great source imagery to create an edgy, gritty pattern. Get out and about and take some digital photos of high rise offices and tower blocks. Look up, down and take pictures from unusual angles.

Uploading images

Upload the photos from your camera. Open the one you wish to use in Photoshop. In View scroll down and make sure Snap To All _is on. Check the image size and make sure it is 300dpi. You can change the size later once you have made the complete pattern unit. Select the image and copy

Select > All
Edit > Copy

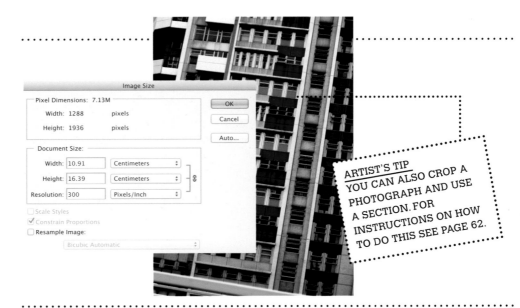

ARTIST'S TIP
YOU CAN ALSO CROP A PHOTOGRAPH AND USE A SECTION. FOR INSTRUCTIONS ON HOW TO DO THIS SEE PAGE 62.

Building a design

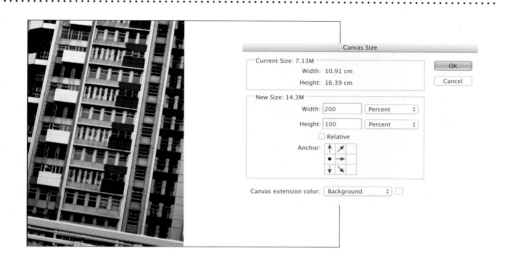

You are going to extend the canvas horizontally.
Image > Canvas Size
In the dialogue box select the middle left hand box. In Width insert 200 percent. Click OK.

Remember that you copied the image at the beginning, now paste it into the extended canvas.
Edit > Paste

Flip horizontally

4

Move the copied image into place; because the Snap to Place is on it will automatically snap into place.

5

With the copied layer selected in the Layers palette, flip the image horizontally.
Edit > Transform > Flip Horizontally
Flatten layers
Layer > Flatten Image

6

Copy the new extended image
Select > All
Edit > Copy
You are going to extend the canvas vertically
Image > Canvas Size
In the dialogue box select the middle top box. In Height insert 200 percent. Click OK.

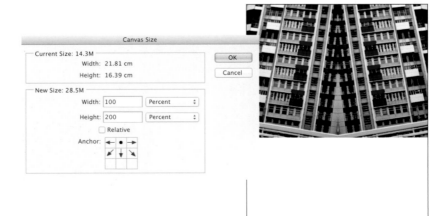

Flip vertically

Remember that you have already copied the flattened image. Now paste into the extended canvas.
Edit > Paste
Snap your design into position.

Move and snap it into place. With the new pasted layer selected in the Layers palette, flip the image vertically.
Edit > Transform > Flip Vertical
Flatten the layers
Layer > Flatten Image
Now the image is in a mirrored repeat unit, you can experiment with some colour adjustments.

Open the Adjustment dialogue box if it is not on your workspace.
Window > Adjustments
Play around with the different options available. When selected a new layer will appear with the adjustment you have chosen to use. Turn Layer Adjustment off to reveal the new layer beneath.

Black & white

10

You will now use the Black and White Adjustment. In the Black and White Properties panel move the vertical sliders to the desired effect. To alter the tone, select Brightness and Contrast option in the Adjustments palette and move the vertical sliders. Once happy
Layer > Flatten Image
Save your design as a Tiff.

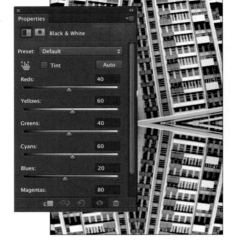

11

Print your design unit on paper and hold it up against yourself to check the scale. At this point you can change the size.
Image > Image Size
In the dialogue box tick Constrain Proportions and Resample Image. Make the Width and Height percentage smaller or larger depending whether you want to enlarge or reduce the image in size.

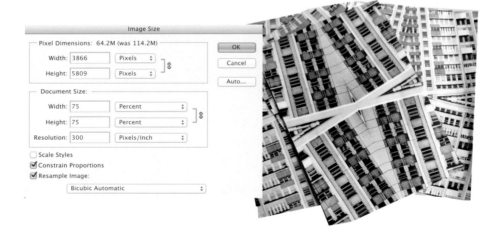

12

Test the design in full repeat.
Edit > Define Pattern
Name your pattern. Open a new document three times bigger than the repeat unit. In this case 150 cm x 150 cm (59 x 59 in)
Edit > Fill
Find your pattern in the Pattern Library, click OK to Fill to see the full effect. Now send your design unit to the printer!

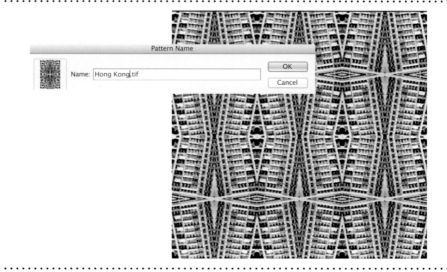

12
***

Stitched by Jane

by Jane Bates

Graphic designer and lover of textile patterns Jane Bates created this lovely design. This tutorial shows you how to create a simple cross stitch motif in Illustrator and put it into a half drop repeat ready to print onto a fresh cotton lawn fabric. For this easywear top we used a Tova sewing pattern by Wiksten.

Getting Started

You'll find cross-stitch inspiration everywhere you look, in tiles, pixelated images, symmetrical designs and sewing books. Making a simple grid and using a pencil to plot designs is the best way to start.

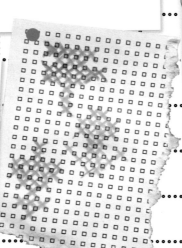

Choose a pattern

This design is inspired by a Japanese vintage cross stitch pattern book by Misako Murayama, referencing a flower motif.

First create a cross stitch canvas. Open Preferences in the option bar and click on Units. Set the General Units to millimetres. Set the Stroke and Type to Millimetres. Click OK. Select the Guides and Grid panel and set your gridline every 3 mm. Click OK.

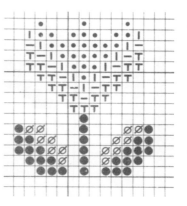

Cross stitch canvas

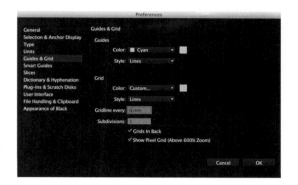

File > New
and change the width and height to 54 mm size.
Click OK.
This will create a grid of 18 x 18 mm squares.

Use even numbers as you will eventually create a half drop repeat with the cross stitch motif.

In the View menu scroll down to Show Grid. Your grid will appear, an 18 x 18 mm square grid ready to build the cross stitch. In View scroll down and Snap to Grid to ensure your cross stitches snap to the grid when you start to draw them.

Line Segment Tool →

Stroke and Fill →

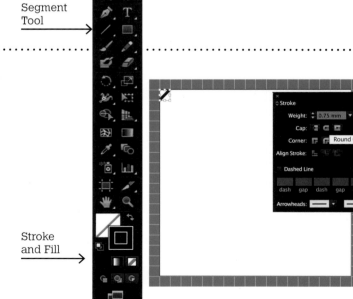

Stroke Weight

In the toolbar set your Stoke to Black and Fill to None. Select the Line Segment tool. In the menu bar click on Stroke. The Stroke panel will appear; change Stroke Weight to 0.75pt and underneath this select Round Cap. In the first grid draw a diagonal line in the first square.

Creating a cross stitch

 6

Draw a second diagonal line over the first. With the Selection tool, select both lines and group together.
Object > Group
Now you will scale so the stitch fits within the grid.
Object > Transform > Scale
Select 70%.

 7

Now you will build a cross stitch grid. Select your first cross stitch with the Selection Tool. Hit Return to bring up the Move dialogue box. Enter 3 mm in the Horizontal field and click Copy. Your second cross stitch will appear.

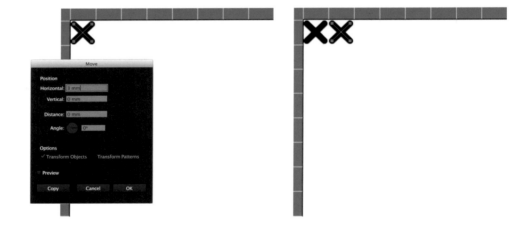

 8

To build the vertical line of crosses, press Command + D to duplicate the last command until you reach the end of the grid.

Cross stitch canvas

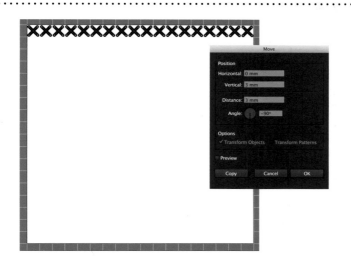

9

To build a vertical line of cross stitches, select all the cross stitches with the selection tool. Press the return key to bring up the Move dialogue box.

Enter 3 mm in the Vertical field and click on Copy. Press Command + D to repeat the command until you get to the bottom of the grid.

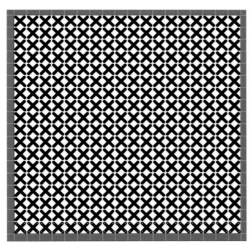

YOU NOW HAVE YOUR CROSS STITCH UNIT READY TO CREATE A MOTIF!

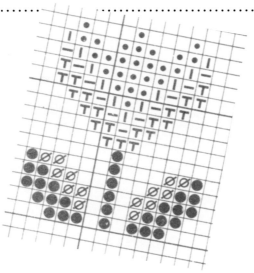

10

Now you will design your cross stitch template pattern. Choose a cross stitch motif that you want to follow. Look through cross stitch pattern books to find ideas for a motif like this vintage flower design.

Making a motif

Working from the centre, select your cross stitches, holding down the Shift key as you go. Follow your reference image to build your motif. Colour this selection with a grey stroke.

NOTE
THE MOTIF IS NOT CENTRED HERE BECAUSE WE WANT TO MAKE IT INTO A HALF DROP REPEAT AND IT IS EASIER TO WORK WITH AN EVEN NUMBERED GRID.

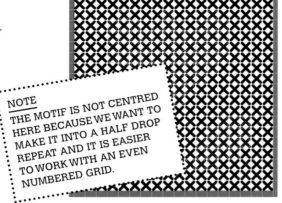
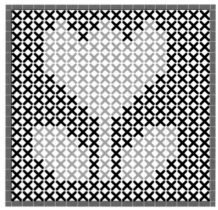

Once you are happy with the motif you can colour the stitches in.

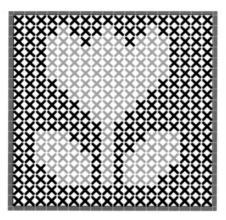
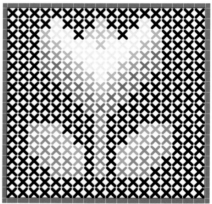

To try a different colour stroke, select a cross stitch. Go to Select in the menu bar, scroll down to **Select > Stroke Colour** and change the colour. Continue to experiment!

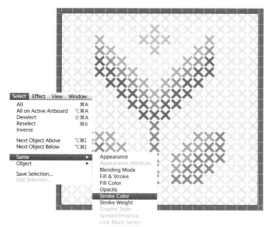

Export to Photoshop

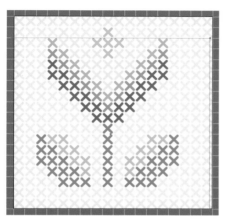
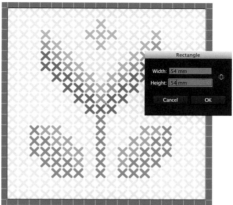

14

To prepare the motif for a half drop repeat you need to put it in a boundary box. Double click the rectangle icon in the toolbar.

Remember the document size is 54 x 54 mm; put in these measurements, click OK. A boundary box will appear. Fill the stoke with none and place over the document box, it should snap to grid. The motif is safely within this box.

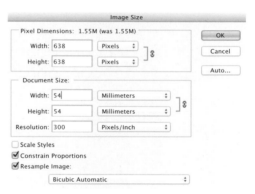

15

Export to Photoshop to put into a half drop repeat unit. In Illustrator, select
File > Export
Find the folder you want to export to and choose Tiff as the file format. Open in Photoshop. Check the image size is correct
Image > Image Size
It should be 54 x 54 mm. Put the Snap To mode on
View > Snap To Grid
Show rulers
View > Rulers

ARTIST'S TIP
DRAG THE RULER TO THE CROSSHAIRS TO FIND THE CENTRE POINT OF THE DESIGN.

16

Next find the centre point of the design.
Select > All
Edit > Free Transform
You will see crosshairs appear. Drag a ruler down so it snaps to the crosshair Hit Escape then
Select > All
Edit > Copy

Half-drop repeat

 17

Now extend the canvas.
Image > Canvas Size
A dialogue box will appear. Select the middle box on the left hand side of the Anchor grid. Enter 200 per cent in the Width field.

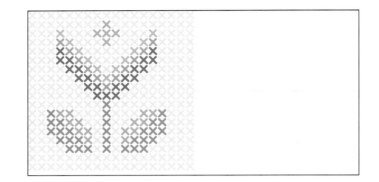

 18

Edit > Paste
Drag the motif below the ruler so it snaps into place. Paste again and move the motif above the ruler so it snaps into place.
Layer > Flatten Image

Your half drop motif is complete!!

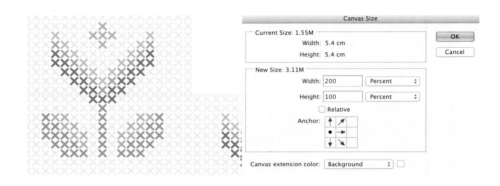

 19

Finally, add colour to individual cross stitches to break up the background by selecting with the Magic Wand and filling with a colour. Your repeat unit is ready to send to the printers.

Magic Wand Tool

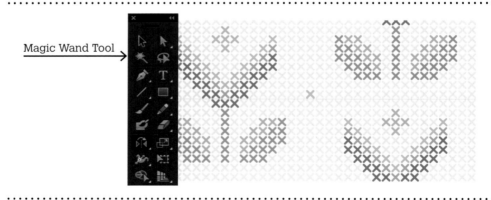

 20

To see your pattern repeat
Edit > Define Pattern
Name your pattern. Open a new document three times larger than the repeat unit. In this case 162 x 162 cm.
Edit > Fill > Pattern
Find your pattern in the pattern library and click OK to see the full repeat.

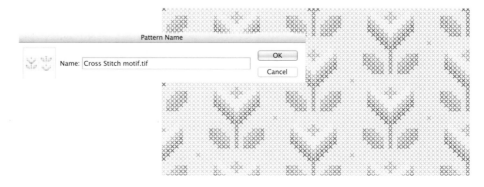

13

***

YOU WILL NEED

digital camera

travel pass, money

laundry bag

garment pattern

Made in Brixton

Designer – Kathyrn Round

Textile designer and Brixton resident Kathyrn Round finds inspiration in the patterns, colours and culture of her local market surroundings. On her travels she photographs textures and images to create electric print combinations are placed into garment pieces, printed onto a bamboo/silk mix and made into a simple sweat top that reflects her love of her surroundings.

Getting Started

If you don't have a local market, look around your neighbourhood. High street stores and street signage can provide dynamic and quirky imagery suitable for print. Take some close-up shots of everyday objects. Choose a theme such as textures, patterns, colour or typography.

Finding a pattern

This is an engineered garment at it's simplest, where you place the image into the pattern shapes. You will place your photos into a simple sweatshirt shape, the Odette top by Fine Motor Skills. This is a boxy, easy top that comes as a downloadable PDF pattern to print and piece together. This pattern is in metric but you can find commercial patterns for sweat tops in Imperial measurements.

the odette top
WITH FREE PATTERN !

FINE MOTOR SKILLS
www.fine-motor-skills.blogspot.ca

Printing pattern pieces

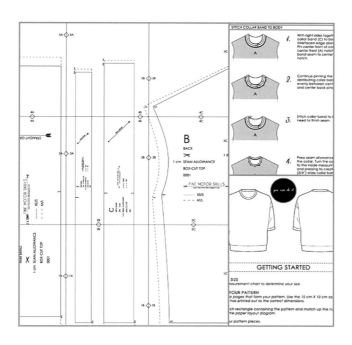

Print out the pattern pieces and measure them to plan which images you want to place where. Print your PDF pattern out following the print instructions, and piece together to make your garment pattern pieces.

The Odette Top is really easy, a back, a front, collar band, sleeves and bottom band. For the collar band you can use an offcut of another fabric as a coloured trim.

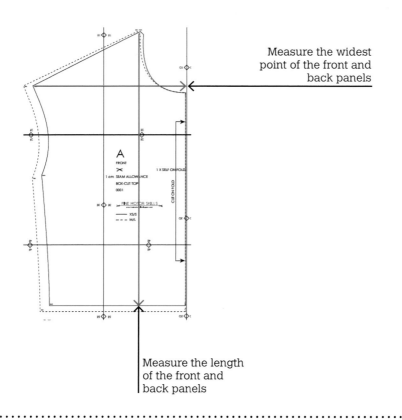

Measure the widest point of the front and back panels

Measure the length of the front and back panels

With the pattern pieces stuck together, measure the width at the widest point of the front panel. The pattern pieces for the front and back panels are half panels, they measure: Width 35 cm and Height 62 cm. Multiply the width measurement twice to get the full panel width (70 cm)

The sleeve panel is 43 cm x 31 cm and the hem band is 60 cm x 15 cm. The collar band is 6 cm x 68 cm. Allow for fabric shrinkage and add an extra 2 cm on all sides.

Preparing document

Now you know the document sizes. Open Photoshop and create a new document 74 cm x 66 cm at 300dpi. This will be the front.

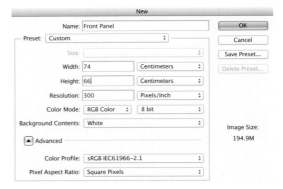

You need to place a guide line to indicate yoke line on the panel. Go to
View > Rulers
The rulers appear along the top and left side of the active window. With the Move tool selected drag a ruler from the left hand side of the window and drag to the centre point of the document. As you drag the ruler the X measurement will show. In this case 37 cm, half of the document size.

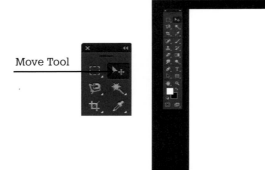

Move Tool

Centre line

Back to your pattern piece, measure from the top of the shoulder to yoke line as indicated on the pattern. In this case it is 23 cm.

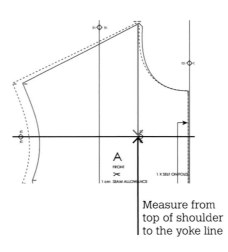

Measure from top of shoulder to the yoke line

Front panel

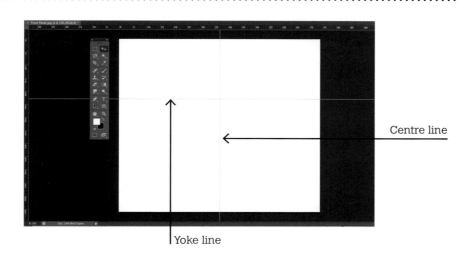

Centre line

Yoke line

In Photoshop, with the Move tool selected, drag a ruler down to mark where the yoke line is on the front panel document. You will have two rulers, the centre point and the yoke line.

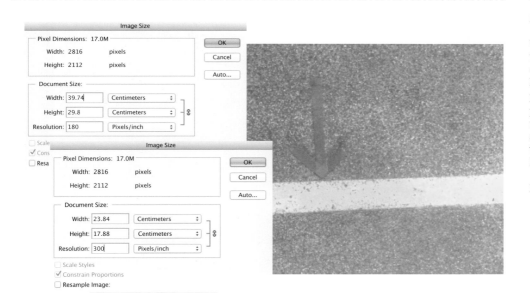

Upload your photos to your computer, select and organise in your Photo Library.

In Photoshop, open the photograph you want to use. Check the image size and change to 300dpi with the Constrain Proportions box ticked.
   Image > Image size
Put in 300dpi.

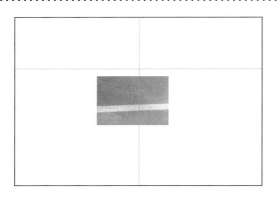

Select and copy the photograph.
   Select > All
   Edit > Copy
Go back to your document for your front panel.
   Edit > Paste
Your photograph will appear on the front panel document.

Front panel

10

You need to scale the image up to flood the document.
Edit > Transform > Scale
A box with anchor angles will appear around the image. On your keyboard, press and hold down the Shift key and drag the right hand anchor handle until the image fits the whole document. Using Shift and Drag will scale the image proportionally within your document.

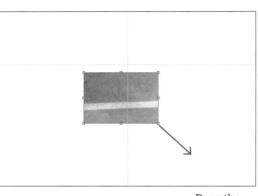

Drag the anchor handle

11

Select the Move Tool and move into place so it fits under the yoke line ruler.

Move Tool

12

We decided to use the check pattern from a zipped plastic laundry bag for this tutorial. Buy a laundry bag and cut a panel out.

Lay the laundry bag on the scanner and scan at 300dpi.

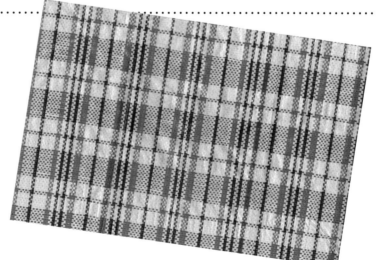

Laundry bag check

Open the new scan in Photoshop
Select > All
Edit > Copy
Now on your front panel
Edit > Paste
Scale to fit the document
Edit > Transform > Scale
Your check will go over the first photograph, therefore we need to place this layer behind to reveal it.

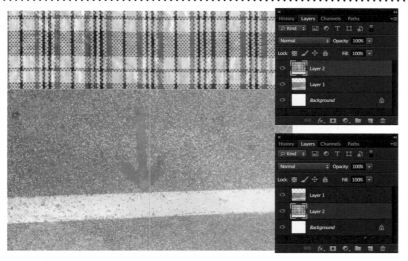

You will have three layers in your Layers palette. Select the new pasted Layer 2 and drag it below Layer 1

Your new image will now be under Layer 1.

Finally, open one more photograph, copy and paste and scale to fit into the top panel.

The front panel is done!

Flatten the layers
Layer > Flatten Image
Save and name your document.

Back panel

 16

Now you are ready to work on the back panel pattern.
File > New > Document
Here, we use photos of a market shutter and another colourway of a laundry bag. Following the same process you used to build the front panel, you will now build the back panel.

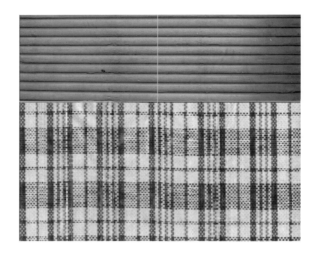

 17

To add a football to the front panel, draw a circle around the football with the Round Marquee tool, holding down the Shift key to keep the proportions. Move the marquee over the football so it fits. Copy the selection.
Edit > Copy

Round Marquee Tool →

 18

Now, on your front panel document, paste the football.
Edit > Paste
With the Move tool, move into place. With the Transform tool scale to fit.
Edit > Transform > Scale
Once you are happy, flatten layers and save.
Layer > Flatten Image

Domino pattern

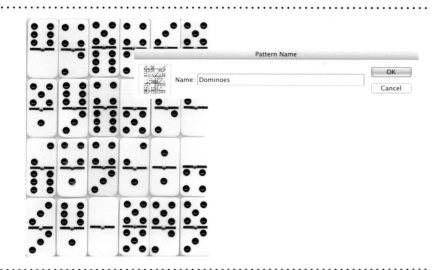

19

A domino pattern creates a fun contrasting design for the sleeves and hem band. Lay the dominoes out and photograph them. Upload the photograph onto your computer.

Open in Photoshop. With the Square Lasso tool select the dominoes.
Edit > Define Pattern
And name 'Dominoes'.

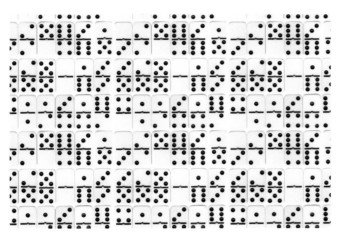

20

Open a new document 47 cm x 35 cm at 300pdi This is the size of the sleeve. We fill the document with the domino pattern to check the repeat.
Edit > Fill > Pattern
Find your domino pattern and click OK. Save your sleeve panel.

Open a new document for the hem band, fill with the domino pattern and save.

21

For the second sleeve we used a photo from Brixton market. Upload and open in Photoshop, making sure the resolution is 300dpi
Select > All
Edit > Copy
Open a second sleeve panel 47 x 35 cm
Edit > Paste
Scale to fit into the document
Edit > Transform > Scale
When happy with the result
Layer > Flatten

Ready to print!

You now have five documents ready to send off to the printers – a front, a back, two sleeves and a hem band. We chose a bamboo/silk mix to print our Made in Brixton top on, and used some contrasting scrap fabric to make the collar band trim.

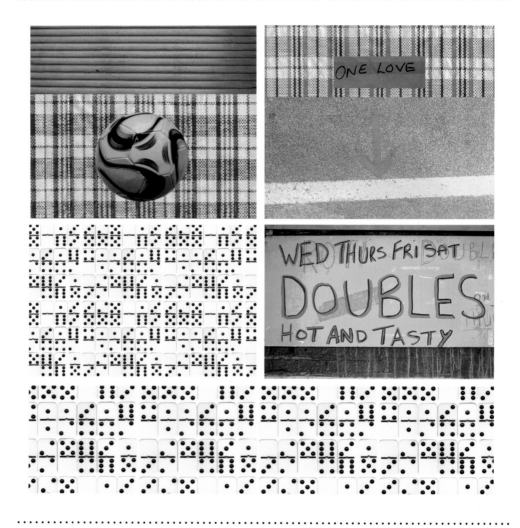

With your fabric back from the printers, lay your pattern piece onto each panel and cut out your garment shapes ready to make.

14

***

YOU WILL NEED

paints and brushes

tracing paper

folk art imagery

paper cutout samples

Modern Folk

Designer – Dr Emma Neuberg

Textile designer and founder of the Slow Textiles Group, Dr Emma Neuberg is passionate about preserving traditional craft techniques and narratives. She shows how to create a stunning scarf design inspired by Northern European paper cutout art that traditionally decorated homes in countries such as Poland, Sweden and Denmark. Using Illustrator, transform your painting into a large bright scarf printed on luxury wool twill.

Getting Started

Research paper cutouts in books and online and you will find some stunning examples of this traditional craft. The paper-cutout term 'Snickeregladje,' means 'fretwork', and these decorative cutout shapes have made many homes happy over the years.

Choosing designs

Working from books or colour printouts, trace and paint elements that will make up your design. You can also use copyright-free books to work from.

The International Design Library®

Folk Art Designs

from Polish Wycinanki and Swiss and German Schere

46

9

by Ramona Jablonski

Creating artwork

With all your favourite paper-cutout printouts and colour photocopies at hand, start tracing elements and create your own variations and colour schemes. Use felt tip pens or acrylic paints on good quality white paper. Painting the artwork gives a hand rendered quality and originality in the final design.

Paint your tracings in different colours so that you'll have lots of variety to develop once they're scanned into the computer.

Scanning the artwork

Now scan in your finished painting. This painting is A3 size, but the scanner we used was A4, so we scanned it in two halves and pasted them together in Photoshop.

Scan in your artwork at 300 dpi and open up the documents in Photoshop. Name and save the first artwork Scan 1 and the second artwork Scan 2.

Go to the Scan 1 to increase the canvas by 200% so you can paste the second part of the artwork to make a complete canvas.

In the Options bar select
Image > Canvas Size
A dialogue box will appear. Select the middle left hand square and put 200 percent in the Width size. Click OK.

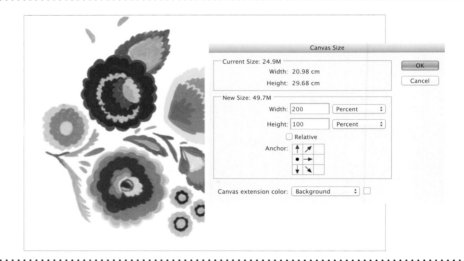

Go to Scan 2 and copy.
Select > All
Edit > Copy

Go back to Scan 1 and paste Scan 2 in the increased canvas size.
Edit > Paste

Preparing artwork

 Move Tool

7

Select the Move tool from the toolbar and carefully move Scan 2 into the new canvas so the two halves fit together.

Once they fit flatten the document. In the Option bar go to
Layers > Flatten Image

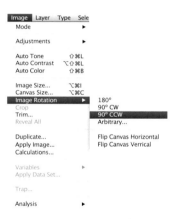

8

To put the document the correct way up, go to the Option bar
Image > Image Rotation > 90° CCW

9

To brighten your image before opening it in Illustrator, go to the Options bar
Image > Adjustments
Select Brightness/Contrast. A dialogue box will appear. Move the sliders of Brightness and Contrast so the background is crisp white. Click OK.

Save your prepared artwork as a Jpeg image.

Ready for Illustrator

10

Next you will convert the painting in Photoshop from a bitmap image into a vector image in Illustrator. This means you can enlarge your artwork to any size and maintain a crisp quality. It also allows paint marks to become clean shapes, giving a graphic cutout feel.

Photoshop Bitmap Image   Illustrator Vector Image

11

Open Illustrator and open the saved Jpeg image. Don't worry if this goes beyond the artboard, you will compose this later. Select the whole image with the Direct Selection tool.

You are now going to convert the image into a vector artwork.

Direct Selection Tool

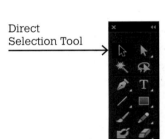

12

Go to Window in the Option bar, scroll down and find Image Trace. The dialogue box will appear.

In the dialogue box set
Preset > Low Fidelity Photo
View > Tracing Results
Palette > Full Tone
Click Trace.

Your image will now look smoother and flatter.

Image trace

Expand

 13

Make the motifs into paths so they can be individually edited. In the Image Tracing Option bar, select Expand; you will see the paths around the motifs.
Image > Ungroup
With the Selection Tool select the outside rectangle and hit Delete. Select all of the image
Select > All
Copy and paste into a new document ready to scale up and arrange.

 14

You are now going to create a new document for the scarf. You want to print the biggest scarf you can.

Check with the printer the maximum print size that you can design to on your choice of fabric. In this case it was 135 cm (54 in) width. So we made the document 135 cm x 135 cm (54 in x 54 in).
File > New

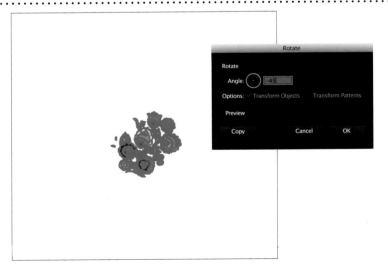

 15

In your new document paste the image that you previously copied.
Edit > Paste
It will appear in the middle of your new canvas

To rotate the image go to the Option bar and select
Object > Transform > Rotate
A dialogue box will appear. Put -45 degree in Angle and click OK.

Scarf layout

16

Enlarge the image to fit the scarf document. To scale the image go to the Option bar and select
Object > Transform > Scale
A dialogue box will appear, put 400% in the Uniform box and select Non Uniform. Click OK. If your design is over the document, select the Scale tool and, holding down the Shift key, scale to fit your image.

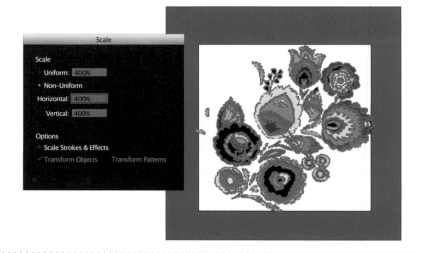

17

Now arrange the motifs and space them out. Select the Direct Selection tool from the toolbar, carefully hover it over the motif to select it and move it to fit in the space. You can always go back to paint some more motifs and add some extra detail. Save your finished scarf design.

18

To export your Modern Folk scarf design
File > Export
Locate where you want to save it and choose a file type (in this case a Tiff). Click OK. A dialogue box will appear. Select RGB in the Colour Model and 200dpi in resolution. Click OK and your design is ready to send to the printer.

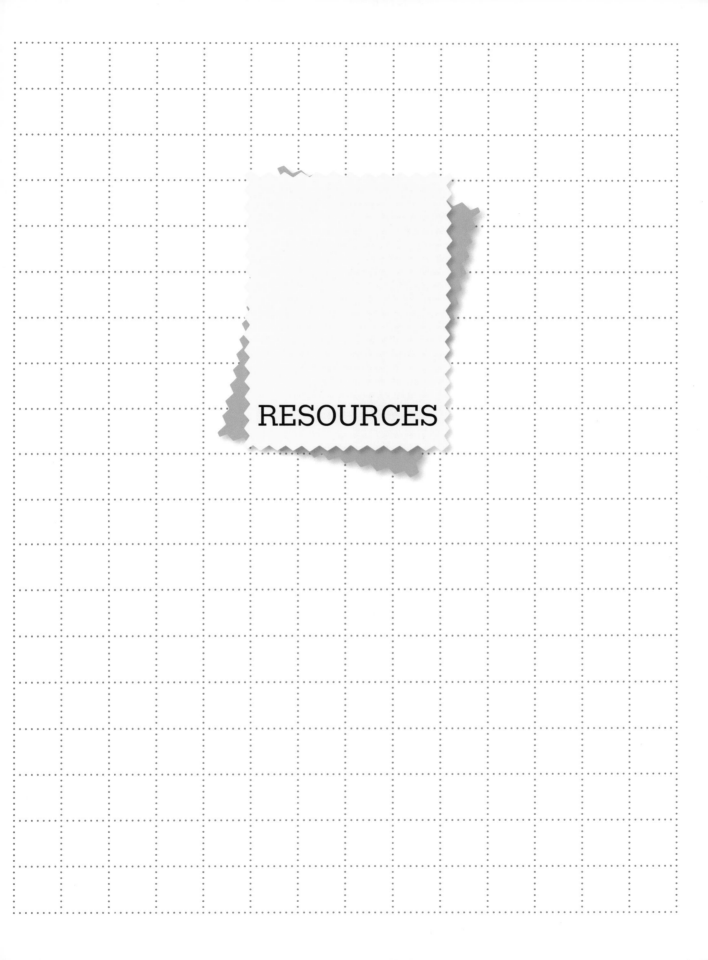

RESOURCES

Digitally printing your fabric

Digital textile printing developed out of technology initially devised for reprographics – printing on paper using large format inkjet printers. Over the last decade we have seen huge advances and investment in this technology, making it possible for textile dyes to be printed onto fabric and providing an alternative to traditional screen printing. Digital printing is now having a huge impact on the textile industry, as well as the consumers who are able to print their own fabrics from the increasing numbers of digital print bureaus. The Smithers Pira marketing report of 2013 predicted that digital textile printing is set to double by 2017, so the future looks bright.

Digital printing has many advantages over traditional printing methods, such as speed, efficiency, fewer design restrictions and lower cost in smaller manufacturing runs. Digital printing offers a wide range of possibilities for the designer because of the ability to print intricate patterns, limitless colours and photographic detail, using any scale or repeat as well as non-repeating and engineered designs. In time this printing method will become the preferred print process, particularly for small runs.

It is now possible to order a small print run, allowing hobbyist enthusiasts as well as professionals to design and print short runs of fabric for prototyping and production, and we are witnessing entrepreneurial businesses flourishing. The turnaround for printing your design can be as little as one or two weeks, and many bureaus offer an easy upload file system, helpful print guidelines and online communities for the creator to show off their product.

Sustainability
Digital inkjet printing has many environmental advantages over traditional printing methods. This is primarily due to less wastage of dye as the ink is printed on demand, and the fabric can be printed as an allover repeat or to specific pattern placements, thereby reducing fabric wastage. Inkjet also uses less water and less electricity. These savings mean that the process has less impact on the environment than traditional print processes, offering a more sustainable future. Choosing a local print bureau means fewer freight miles and a reduced carbon footprint. Some printers offer printing onto eco–fabrics such as organic cottons and linens, hemp mixes, bamboo and recycled polyesters. And digital print technology is always advancing, with sustainability at the forefront of its development.

Print and fabric choice
There are two methods used for inkjet printing of textiles. Direct inkjet printing uses inks, which are compatible with silks, cottons, jerseys, and wools. This method uses reactive or acid dyes. Direct printing is more expensive because of the type of fabrics and post-printing processes. Direct printing is printed using an inkjet printer, and printed in as little as a metre or hundreds. Pigment inks are rapidly being used in digital printing, which demand less post process as they dye and fix easily on the cloth and therefore can be a more commercial and economical option. Indirect inkjet printing (sublimation printing) uses disperse dyes for printing on polyester-based fabrics, linoleum and formica. This is a popular process for novelty products. Sublimation printing uses a cheaper substrate and is growing in

popularity for use in personalized products, where photographs are used on products such as bags, t-shirts and soft furnishings.

All digitally printed fabric dyes are permanently fixed, so your fabric can be machine- or hand washed depending on the fabric you have chosen. The projects in this book focus on creating designs to be printed by bureaus which offer direct inkjet technology and use inks which can printed onto an increasing range of natural fabrics.

Using a print bureau

You can choose your print bureau by recommendation, by locality and by the service and choice of fabrics they print on. All print bureaus will have information online and will offer to send you a swatch book of fabrics they use for printing. Some print bureaus offer a service purely online to upload your design, which they will post to you once printed. It's good to build up a relationship with the bureau so you understand the range of fabrics and service that they provide and specialize in.

Preparing your file

The print bureau will give you information on how to prepare your file and what format they need it in and how to get the artwork to them. Be sure to follow their instructions as extra artworking time required by them can add an additional cost. Most printers require a flattened Tiff file in either RGB or Lab Colour with a resolution of no more than 300dpi at the size the design is to be printed. All artwork is sent to scale. If you have a

repeat you just need to send the repeat unit, as they will have the software to fill the fabric with the amount that you require. Most inkjet printers print fabrics with a width of 140 cm (55 inches). Remember to check all information and guidelines with the print bureau.

Colour

The most common question a printer is asked is 'can you match my screen colour to my print colour'? The colour from your screen may differ from the bureau's screen and may not be reproduced exactly. Colour can also vary from one substrate to the next. All bureaus have advanced colour management software, which a professional large textile studio will employ, but for the small scale printer/designer it is best to order a colour test before placing a large order to help you determine whether your colours will print as expected. Always ask advice from the printer on how to get the best colour match for your printed textile.

Digital print communities

More and more bureaus are now building buzzing communities through the service they provide. Social media allows you to showcase your creative work and provides support, tutorials, competitions and forums. This offers an exciting option for small-scale entrepreneurs to sell and promote their work through an online community.

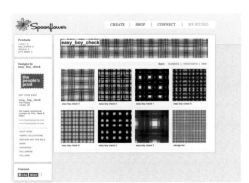

Far left
Printing the fabric for the Easy Boy Check shirt.

Left
Screengrab showing the fabrics packaged using Spoonflower software, ready to go to the printer.

Making your garment

Over the last decade there has been a sewing revival and a growing interest in people making their own clothes. We are witnessing a backlash against fast fashion on the high street and mass consumerism, with today's consumer being more ethically conscious of where their clothes are made and who has made them. The sales in sewing machines have rocketed alongside the growth in technology. We crave to balance the technology with the need for a physical and emotional investment in our products. It's time to embrace the Slow Movement, making connections with the craft of creating, sewing and making, and taking satisfaction in what you wear.

Sewing requires time and patience but it clearly engages the maker/wearer with their own product, giving them pride and a sense of fulfilment. It allows for personal customization, creating a bespoke and unique product for the wearer. Imagine creating your own fabric design and making your own garment too! Imagine creating a garment that is totally unique, without thousands of copies on the high street. Imagine having a garment that has your story embedded so that it is totally original to you. This garment surely would have a longer life and become a treasured item rather than a throwaway fashion piece, and even be passed down through the generations as vintage handmade clothing has been.

Choosing a pattern

There are lots of established dressmaking pattern companies to choose from, both online or in craft stores. But there is also a new breed of pattern company that offers a more contemporary, clean look that keeps up with trends and caters to the style savvy dressmaker. These companies often provide downloadable patterns that you can print out and piece together to make your pattern pieces, as well as online communities sharing tips and original ideas. The internet is also bursting with sewing bloggers and communities that post pictures of the clothing creations they have made, testing patterns and sharing advice.

Look at your favourite stores for pattern shapes that inspire as well as suit you. Or just look in your own wardrobe for favourite items of clothing to self-draft a pattern using the DIY couture technique of pattern cutting. The pattern you choose will tell you the level of expertise required. If you are a novice choose an easy pattern. I recommend that you make a practise toile in inexpensive material before using your specially printed fabric, as you are investing time and commitment in your garment. Once you have a perfect pattern you can repeat it several times with a different print.

How and where to learn to sew

The growing interest in handcrafts in recent years has produced a boom in inspiring teaching material, local sewing classes, online tutorials and forums to provide support for the 21st century seamstress. Even TV programmes such as 'The Great British Sewing Bee' in the UK, have fuelled the curiosity of a new generation who were previously not taught to sew.

If you are new to sewing, check out your local adult education centre for dressmaking classes where you can learn to sew with technical guidance. We have also seen the arrival of enterprising and thriving 'sewing cafes' or 'parlours' offering classes, encouragement and support as well as space and sewing machines, while meeting other enthusiasts over a cup of coffee in a social environment.

And if you really don't want to make your own clothes but want something truly original then there are plenty of seamstresses who would be happy to sew your project for you for a fee. Just check out your local haberdashery store for contacts and recommendations.

Which fabric?

There is a large choice of fabrics available to digitally print on, offering different weights of cottons, jerseys, silks and linens, these fabrics are often better quality than fabrics used in high street stores. I suggest that you check your local digital print bureau first to see what fabrics they provide, asking to see their swatch book. Each bureau has

a different range and particular expertise, some focusing on silks and top-end fabrics while others may focus on fabrics more often used by amateurs such as cotton poplins, lawns and twills. Cottons and linens are the easiest fabrics to sew and the cheapest fabrics to print, and are easy to care for. To work with silks and jersey you need to be experienced and practised in using them

Take it slow! Sewing takes time!

Sewing requires thought, patience, concentration and time. You will go through the process of making errors and working them out, and this will add to the attachment to your garment and give you pride in learning, making and wearing. Remember that you will wear your handmade garment for many years so your investment of time will be rewarded.

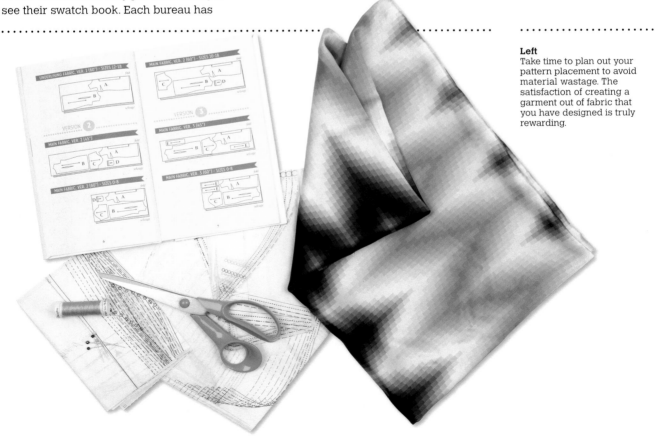

Left
Take time to plan out your pattern placement to avoid material wastage. The satisfaction of creating a garment out of fabric that you have designed is truly rewarding.

Independent pattern designers

By Hand London
www.byhandlondon.com

Center For Pattern Design
www.centerforpatterndesign.com

Colette Patterns
www.colettepatterns.com

Christine Haynes
www.christinehaynes.com

Deer and Doe
www.boutique.deer-and-doe.fr

Deuxieme Arrondissement
www.deuxiemearrondissement.com

Dixie DIY
www.dixiediy.blogspot.co.uk

DIY Couture
www.diy-couture.co.uk

Favourite Things
www.favoritethings.net

Fine Motor Skills
www.fine-motor-skills.blogspot.ca

Garmenter
www.garmenter.com

Grain Line Studio
www.grainlinestudio.com

In House Patterns
www.inhousepatterns.com

Jamie Christina
www.jamiechristina.com

Kate and Rose
www.kate-and-rose.com

Made By Rae
www.made-by-rae.com

Make It Perfect
www.makeitperfect.com.au

Megan Nielsen
www.megannielsen.com

Merchant and Mills
www.merchantandmills.com

Miy Collection
www.miycollection.co.uk

Nette
www.nettevivante.blogspot.co.uk

Paper Cut Patterns
www.papercutpatterns.com

Pattern Runaway
www.patternrunway.com

Pauline Alice
www.paulinealicepatterns.com

Salme Sewing Patterns
www.etsy.com/shop/Salmepatterns

Seamingly Smitten
www.etsy.com/shop/seaminglysmitten

Seamster
www.seamsterpatterns.com

Sew Aholic
www.sewaholic.net

Sew Caroline
www.sewcaroline.com

Sewing Workshop
www.sewingworkshop.com

Sew Over It
www.sewoverit.co.uk

Sew Square One
www.sewnsquareone.com

Sinbad and Sailor
www.sinbadandsailor.com

Sis Boom
www.sisboom.com

The Makers Journal
www.etsy.com/shop/themakersjournal

Thread Theory Design Inc
www.threadtheory.ca

Tilly and the Buttons
www.tillyandthebuttons.com

Victory Patterns
www.victorypatterns.com

Wiksten
www.shopwiksten.com

Commercial pattern designers

Butterick Patterns
www.butterick.mccall.com

Burda
www.burdastyle.com

Kwik Sew
www.kwiksew.mccall.com

McCALL Patterns
www.mccallpattern.mccall.com

New Look
www.simplicitynewlook.com

Simplicity
www.simplicity.com

Vogue
www.voguepatterns.mccall.com

Digital print bureaus for small print runs

UK

Bags of Love
www.bagsoflove.co.uk

Be Fab Be Creative
www.befabbecreative.co.uk

By Hand London
www.byhandlondon.com

Centre for Advanced Textiles
www.catdigital.co.uk

Citrus Rain
www.citrus-rain.com

Digetex
www.digetex.com

&digital
www.anddigital.co.uk

FabPad
www.uel.ac.uk/fabpad

Fancy Prints
www.fancyprints.co.uk

Fashion Digital Studio
http://fashiondigitalstudio.com

Finger Print
www.fingerprintfabric.com

Forest Digital
www.forestdigital.co.uk

Hatley Print Ltd
www.hatleyprint.co.uk

HTS Print and Design
www.htsprint.co.uk

J.A.Gillmartin
www.camerongilmartin.co.uk

Liberty Press
www.libertypress.co.uk

L&S Prints Digital Ltd
www.lsprints.co.uk

Magic Textiles Ltd
www.magictextiles.co.uk

Pretty Me Print
www.printmepretty.co.uk

RA Smart Ltd
www.rasmart.co.uk

Silk Bureau
www.silkbureau.co.uk

Surface Pattern Print
www.surfacepatternprint.com

The Fabric Press
www.thefabricpress.com

The Woven Monkey
www.wovenmonkey.com

USA

Advanced Digital Textiles
www.advdigitaltextiles.com

Art of Where
http://artofwhere.com

CadFab
http://cadfab.net

Dream Fabric Printing
www.dreamfabricprinting.com

Dye-Namix
www.dyenamix.com

Fabric on Demand
www.fabricondemand.com

First2Print
www.first2print.com

Modern Yardage
www.modernyardage.com

Spoonflower
www.spoonflower.com

Super Sample
www.supersample.com

Surface Pattern Print
www.surfacepatternprint.com

CANADA

Silk Melody
http://silkmelody.com

AUSTRALIA

Digital Fabric Printer
www.digitalfabricprinter.com.au

Digital Fabrics
www.digitalfabrics.com.au

Frankie and Swiss
www.frankieandswiss.com.au

CONTINENTAL EUROPE

Bergh Fabrics
www.berghfabrics.com

Circulo Textil
www.circultextil.com

Motif Personnel
www.motifpersonnel.com

Stoffn
www.stoffn.de

Stoff Schmie
www.stoff-schmie.de

Textile Fab
www.textilefab.de

Acknowledgments & credits

Thanks to my dear friend and talented graphic designer Jane Bates for designing and making such a beautiful and special book with me.

Further thanks to Jane Walker for making all of the garments in the book so beautifully and being so generous with her time, skill and enthusiasm. Thanks to Rosie Martin, of *DIY Couture*, for styling a fantastic photo shoot and being an inspiring part of the DIY movement; Dr Emma Neuberg, co-founder of The People's Print, for her passion for textile design; Kathryn Round for her daily optimism and creativity; Caryn Simonson for her support; Textile Futures Research Centre for their backing; Lynne Searl for her assistance; the students and staff from Chelsea College of Art and Design for all of their inspiration.

Special thanks, to my partner Philip Dolman for his support and belief in my work and to my children Ben, Eve and Maya.

Thank you to the editors at Laurence King Publishing, Helen Rochester, Sue George and Gaynor Sermon, for believing whole heartedly in the book.

My thanks to the digital print bureaus for printing the fabrics: Jacqui Gilmartin at JA Gilmartin; Alan Shaw at the Centre for Advanced Textiles, Glasgow School of Art; Magnus Mighall at RA Smart; Doug and Elaine Davies at The Silk Bureau; Zoe and Solii at BeFab Be Creative; Kenny Taylor, Chelsea College of Art and Design; Spoonflower; Nerys Mathias at Fabpad.

Contributors

Ruth Esmé Mitchell, Clara Vuletich, Joanna Fowles, Nina Chakrabarti, Kathryn Round, Henry Muller, Emma Neuberg, Jane Bates. Nail art for Colour Me In by Isabella Rocha.

Patterns

The Paintbrush Floral: Tilly and the Buttons – Picnic Skirt
Post Modern Play: The Elise T – Fine Motor Skills
Easy Boy Check: Colette – Negroni Shirt
Vintage Floral College: Burda 7072
Hackney Lights: Simplicity 1887
Bargello Dress: Colette Patterns – Laurel
Patchwork Shirt: Colette – Ginger
Digital Shibori: DIY Couture
Colour Me In: Cut from model's own PJs
Monotone Man: Burda – Amin 6029
Stitched by Jane: Wiksten Pattern – Tova
Made in Brixton: Fine Motor Skills – The Odette Top

The author

Melanie Bowles is a textile designer, co-founder of The People's Print, and senior lecturer on the BA (Hons) course in Digital Textile Design at Chelsea College of Art and Design, London. She has previously published *Digital Textile Design*.

Picture credits

Models and clothing photography
Photographer: Simon Pask Photography
www.simonpask.com
Stylist: Rosie Martin
Models: Maya Dolman-Bowles, Skye Williams, Rikiya Koike, Hannah Jordan, Naomi Bailey-Cooper
Makeup and hair: Karen Fundell; Haleigh Maskall @ HMS Creative

Paintbrush Floral
Joan Red (sandals) by Esska
www.esskashoes.com

Post-Modern Play
Raven Shorts (sewing pattern) by Sinbad & Sailor
www.sinbadandsailor.com

Dahlia Skirt
Bangle Blacks (boots) by Hudson
www.hudsonshoes.com

Hackney Lights
Glasses and ring by Kitty Joseph
www.kittyjoseph.com
Luna Blacks by Miista
http://miista.com

Made in Brixton
Item: High Cut Flash Trainers by Eley Kishimoto
www.eleykishimoto.com

Modern Folk
Monet Cardigan by Eley Kishimoto
www.eleykishimoto.com

Clara's Patchwork Shirt
Satchel by Cambridge Satchel Company
www.cambridgesatchel.com

Bargello Dress
Vintage Shoes by Circus Brixton
www.circusbrixton.com

Inspiration board photography
Ida Riveros